FIND

A

DIME

Maria Sweetman

ISBN 978-1-68517-597-9 (paperback)
ISBN 978-1-68517-598-6 (digital)

Christian Faith Publishing
832 Park Avenue
Meadville, PA 16335
www.christianfaithpublishing.com

Printed in the United States of America

To my beautiful dad,
For all the love he has sent me from heaven.
You have strengthened my soul.

Hello! My name is Maria, and I live in the great state of Arizona with my domestic partner Geo and my cat Utah.

Introduction

I have always felt a connection to the spiritual world. As a child, I remember seeing the Blessed Mother appear to me at the foot of my bed and then quickly disappear. It was not until many years later when my dad had passed that I started seeing signs everywhere, which was confirmation for me that there is a spirit world and that angels are all around us.

My first spiritual sign that my father sent me was in the hospital room an hour after his passing. The priest was giving him his last rights when I saw a smoky white formation leave his body and slowly passed by all who were in the room (my mother, sister, brother, aunt, uncle, and a new friend that he had made while being hospitalized) and then proceeded to go out the window. Once there, it went straight up, and I knew my father's soul went to heaven on that day, January 9, 1991. I was the only one to witness this.

My second spiritual sign was when we got home that evening; my mother was calling all of his siblings in Italy to tell them of his passing, and while she was on the phone, the oven clock that had never worked in all the years we were living there suddenly started making a very loud screaming sound at the same time that both the hands of the clock are spinning backward superfast. This lasted for about one minute and then went silent. We all witnessed this (my mother, sister, brother, aunt, uncle, and I).

My third spiritual sign was that every time my mother and I would return from visiting my father's resting place, and we were pulling up into the driveway, a very large raven would be sitting where my father would always sit and have his evening espresso and a cigarette. This event happened repeatedly every single time we would go to see him, and the first month after his passing, we were visiting him every week, if not more, and that was the beginning of how the raven became a symbol of love from my father to me. The raven has been a part for my life for over thirty years and always shows up at significant times in my life, and I know that my father is bringing him to me. The raven always comforts me.

My father was also communicating with me in dreams. I could ask him a question, and later in my dreams, he would answer the question. He even surprised me with my first three pregnancies. When I became pregnant with my first child, I told my father in prayer that I was sad that he could not be here to witness this and be a part of the baby's life. I also told my husband at the time that I did not want to know the sex of the baby. I wanted it to be a surprise. My father came in my dreams for each of my first three pregnancies all at the end of my first trimester and told me the sex of the baby. I was so happy that he was a part of this special time in my life, and he was correct all three times—confirmation that he is with me in spirit. Angels are amazing; my father is amazing. This went on for years and years. What a blessing from heaven.

One day, I was at work, and a manager shared a spiritual story with me that I will never forget. She told me of her mother's passing, and soon after, she started to find dimes. They were showing up everywhere and even had special meaning to each dime found, like when she went to see her daughter's new house. As they pulled into the driveway and opened the car door, there she found a dime on the asphalt, or the time that she and her siblings were getting ready to cook their first Thanksgiving meal without their mother, and when she went to separate the pans that were stored inside the bottom drawer of the oven, she found a dime, and she knew that her mother was there in spirit. She even told me to look up spiritual meaning of dimes, so I did and this is what I found.

> The number 10 is considered a holy number and historically finding money has represented the presence of a loved one and they are still looking after you. Another fact that has been noted is that people tend to find dimes when they are in a difficult point in their lives and a dime can also be a symbol of confirmation with decisions. (By staff writer)

A few weeks later, it all started. One evening, when I went out for my daily walk, I had the urge to pray again that day. Our family was going through a hard time; my boyfriend at the time had broken his leg in two places, and he was going to be out of work for months. We had five kids to support, and he was the breadwinner. He was already out on leave for two months for a surgery he was healing from when he decided to go for a walk with our youngest son and me. It had rained earlier in the day, and as he led us into the woods, he turned around and told us to be careful because the rain had made everything slippery. As soon as he said this, he slipped while he stepped on top of a tree log that was lying in his path. You could hear his screams for miles. Ambulance had to find us in the woods and transport him to the ER where he had to have emergency surgery right away.

As the weeks went by and he was healing, money became tighter and tighter. He was getting short-term disability, which was only 60 percent of his pay, and I was still bringing home a small paycheck to support us. I thought about everything and the possibility of even losing our home. I chose this house for two reasons: it was only minutes away from mother's home, whose needs I took care of, and it was yellow, my favorite color.

I set out on my daily walk, and I began to talk to God. I told him I was scared, and I was afraid of losing everything that we had worked so hard for. I was also scared for our children. We had five children in the home to support. Also not being close to my mother's home would also hurt.

As I continued to walk and worry, I asked God and my dad to pray for us, and as I was walking, something shiny caught my eye in the grass where it met the sidewalk. As I looked a little bit closer, I saw that it was a dime, and that's how my dime stories began.

Over the years, my spirituality has grown to where I am receiving more visual validations. So one day, I decided to keep a journal for myself of all the special moments that I shared with the spirit world, and one day when I was old, I would sit down and read them. Well, that changed when over the years, I have told family, friends, coworkers, and even strangers of an occurrence that was so beautiful and special that I wanted to share it with someone, and over the many years, I have gotten the same response of "You should write a book."

"You should write a book." It wasn't until many years later, that I got it. It finally sunk in; the angels are speaking to me through humans. I need to write a book! So I wrote a book. A book that captures my spiritual journey over the years.

Raven Sings, Angelo Gets Hearing Aids

October 5, 2001

At the age of five, we were told that Angelo had failed his hearing test at school and to follow up with a hearing specialist. After more tests were done to confirm this diagnosis, we were told to see an ENT-otolaryngologist (ear, nose, and throat doctor). The doctor explained to us that he would need ear tubes, which would have to be surgically implanted, and it would also require putting him under anesthesia. So we had the surgery done, and when my son awoke, the first thing he said to me was, "Mom, I hear you." That brought me to tears. As we exited the surgical center, my mom, son, and I proceeded to the car, and a raven flew up to us and started singing, and I knew it was a sign from my father that he was with us.

Dime at MVA for Angelo

June 15, 2015

Today I took Angelo to the MVA to get his learner's permit. I was a little worried that he was not going to pass. We received our paperwork and proceeded to the counter to fill it out. As I looked forward and down, I saw a dime, and I said, "Angelo, look, it's a dime."

Angelo was so happy he said, "Good, now I know I am going to pass the test!"

I love you, Dad. Thank you for being here. I believe; I believe. Yes, I took a picture. Angelo passed his learner's permit test.

Water Stain Angel

July 8, 2015

We went over to Mrs. Ray's home so Geo could quote her a price on installing a fan in her bedroom. As she was walking us through her home, she accidentally stepped on the dog's water bowl, causing it to tip over and spill all over the place. Upon looking at the stain, I could see an angel; the angel appeared to be standing at a side angle, one wing totally exposed the other way up top, and I quickly told Mrs. Ray her husband is here in spirit. She noticed it too. This was confirmation for Mrs. Ray and I that Mr. Jim crossed over. Mr. Jim had passed a few weeks earlier.

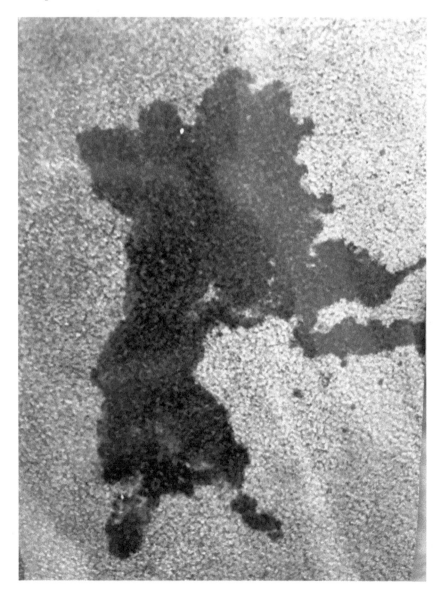

Found a Dime

July 18, 2015

I wanted to say my prayers today in my native language, Italian, so that my father could listen in and understand me speaking with Jesus. I then finished and arrived to work. As I started to walk in, one of my coworkers joined me. It's a long walk to the building, and it is dark because we are scheduled for the 5:00 a.m. shift. As we are walking in, I looked down, and there it was a dime! I was so happy that my father had listened to my prayers. I had to tell my coworker! I love you, Dad!

Crow and Rainbow

October 14, 2015

As I was checking in Frito-Lay, I could hear the crow singing twice to get my attention, so I moved the thermal curtain flaps to see him, and he just flew away. I finished with Frito-Lay, and I walked him out, and with the bright sun out, it started to rain hard, and I knew there was going to be a rainbow, and seconds later, there it was, so big and beautiful. I called out to the Frito-Lay rep who was on his way to his truck to tell him to look at the rainbow, but the rain was so loud that he could not really hear me, so I pointed to the sky, and he finally saw it. My father was sending me a rainbow, and the raven was his messenger.

Stiff Neck

October 16, 2015

This morning, I came to work with a stiff neck. I almost called out, but I am stubborn. Well, today, along with my daily counts, I was asked to count heavy stuff, and I was sad because of my condition of my neck, I would not be able to do so. I said, "A little of help from the angels, and they sent me an angel to help me." One of my overnight managers out of the blue walked by and offered to help me. Angels are amazing. I was then able to do all my counts that day. Thank you, angels. Power of prayer is amazing.

New Car for Priscilla

November 6, 2015

Today, Priscilla got a brand-new Honda Civic. I kept looking for signs of my father. I wanted to see a dime or something. My credit score was just perfect; one point lower, and I would not be approved and therefore not able to help my daughter, who did not have any transportation. When everything was finalized and the tags were issued, the letters on the tags read, "CG," my father's initials backward. Giuseppe Cimino. My father was here. I love you, Dad.

Angel Pendant

November 12, 2015

We arrived in Atlantic City for a little getaway adventure. As we were waiting in line to check in, something shiny caught my eye on the floor from a distant. We were next to be called, so I waited. Then it happened; the next available rep that called us over was the rep that was closest to the shiny object next to the floor. Angels are amazing. As I now was able to see what that shiny object was because I was standing right in front of it. OMG, it's an angel pendant, and I knew that the angel were among us.

Atlantic City False Psychic, Found a Dime

November 13, 2015

I told Geo that the psychic ripped me off $40 but would get it back as soon as I said that we found a dime on the boardwalk. We are in Atlantic City for a few nights, and now tonight, we were at Boogie Nights, dancing when we stepped out for a moment because Geo needed a break, and he sat down at a slot machine, put $20 in, and the machine gave it right back but let him play for free with a $20 credit! He said he had *never* ever saw this in his life. He won $28 free money. That's some of the money I lost because of the psychic. Then Geo put in another $20, thinking maybe he can do it again, but this time, it kept $20 so we needed help getting the $20 out. A man by the name of Joseph (which is *Giuseppe* in Italian and also my father's name) came to help us. We got the $20 back, and I found a quarter, and I thought of how much more we would need to get to $40. It was $12, and as soon as I thought that Geo said, "What number do you think will hit the roller wheel?" And it was twelve! The amount we need to get our total $40 back. We then walked away, and I found a dime; my father was amazing.

Found a Dime

November 16, 2015

I went to see my father today, and after I finished talking to him, I said it would be neat if I found dime near my car in the cemetery. I proceeded to my car and no dime. I then went to get prenatal pills for Vanessa, gas, and a lottery ticket. When I returned to the car, there it was, so shiny, the sun hit it perfectly—a dime, and I knew my father heard me. I love you, Dad.

Happy Birthday Balloon

December 12, 2015

It's my birthday, and I want to celebrate it in Atlantic City.

I want to go eat at the famous all-you-can-eat seafood buffet and then go dancing all night at Boogie Nights. I am so excited too because every birthday I receive a special message from my father. We get there, and it took four hours instead of the normal three hours because of heavy traffic, and we were both tired from the drive, so once in the room, Geo asked me, "What do you want to do know?"

I was tired, so I told him, "Let's take a little nap to refresh ourselves before heading out to dinner." I didn't set an alarm because I did not think we were going to sleep that long; boy was I wrong! We both woke up at 11:30 p.m., and boy was I upset with myself. We missed dinner hour, and I didn't receive a sign from my father yet, and it was only thirty minutes till the next day. Geo suggested we have something small to eat and then go dancing, but for me, the evening was over. So we went downstairs, grabbed subs from the food court, and then we proceeded to go back to our room. Geo felt bad and said, "Let's get up super early and watch the sunrise tomorrow."

I was still a little down because I never not received a sign from my father on my birthday, but Geo is always right, so I agreed. We set the alarm and went to sleep. The next morning, what a beautiful December morning; it was in the seventies, unseasonably warm, and the beautiful sun was just coming up. Geo and I started walking the beach; we walked about one-fourth of a mile before turning around, and as we are walking back, Geo noticed a deflated balloon on the sand floor with the words HAPPY BIRTHDAY written on it, and the only thing that is holding it down is a little bit of wet sand and water that is laying on the creases of the balloon. Geo looked at me and said, "Wow, if that's not a sign, I don't know what is," and I knew it was a sign from my father to me from heaven. He was wishing me happy birthday.

Angels are amazing.

Find a Dime

January 4, 2016

Went to 707 (our address number)—hot! Robert never helps out with anything, and to make matters worse, I was running late for a therapy appointment because Skyler had to go to the bank. All along, Robert is in his room with both doors locked! When I came back to drop off Skyler, he told me Robert's girlfriend was there. I saw the car and went in. I was so angry with him because he never helped out his own kids, and now there is a woman in his room while his kids needed him, and he is never there to help them. We got into a tug-of-war with the bedroom door. I was too strong for him, so he could not close the door on me, and I was yelling at him for being such a lousy dad, and then I grabbed my sun mirror and left. It felt so good. I felt great inside. I then drove to therapy. As I was lying on the massage table and was finishing up therapy, the man lying next to me on another table dropped some change, and sure enough, a dime flew and landed right next to me, and I knew it was definitely my beautiful father confirming what just happened earlier. He was comforting me. I love him so much.

Twenty-Sixth Anniversary of Dad's Passing

January 8, 2016

Went to see my father today; tomorrow will be twenty-six years that he has been gone. After visiting his gravesite, I decided to head to the deli shop, and when I walked in, the song "Volare" by Dean Martin was playing, who also sounds identical to my father, and I knew my father was with me. "Volare" is a song that my father used to sing all the time when we were kids and the word *volare* means fly.

Acid Angel

January 26, 2016

While working on the receiving dock, I noticed a beautiful white angel on the floor. She looked as though she was floating in midair and looking up. I can see her wings too. She looked so magical. I can feel her in my soul. I was wondering how she got there and for how long has she been there. She is next to where we station our forklifts, along with our battery chargers, and probably one of the forklift batteries had leaked acid, and it got on the floor, creating this spectacular creation. I was so mesmerized by this vision of beauty, I had to say a prayer to her. I know she is watching over me. Amen…

Over the many years after seeing this vision, I have shown so many of my coworkers and truck drivers who believe. Angels are amazing. Yes, I took a picture.

Penelope in the Sky

March 10, 2016

A beautiful female angel appeared to me in the early morning sky. She was so beautiful, simply breathtaking; I could not take my eyes off her. The sky looked so magical as it glowed shades of orange, pink, and blue. My first thought was Penelope (my spirit guide). One of my vendors was approaching me when I told him to look at the sky, and if he could see the angel too, but he could not see her, and she was as clear as day. It must have been for only my eyes to see. Yes, I took a picture. I believe that is the very first time I saw Penelope. Angels are amazing.

Maria

March 17, 2016

At 12:57 a.m., while in a deep sleep, I heard my name being called. It was clear as day. It was Penelope. Earlier in my prayers that morning, I had prayed to be able to communicate with the other side by sound. I want to learn to be able to hear her. Then later that day on my lunch break, I had asked Penelope once again to call out my name.

Raven Cloud Visits

March 18, 2016

I am on my lunch break, and as usual, I love to go outside and walk. As I am walking, I noticed a cloud raven watching over me, and I know it is being sent by my father. I can clearly see its eye socket, beak, body, tail, and feet as clear as clear can be. Thank you, Dad, for loving me. Yes, I took a picture.

Ravens, Ravens, Ravens

March 21, 2016

I heard the raven calling. I went outside, and there they were four ravens on the building singing, and then I saw a whole bunch more of them; they were everywhere circling around and around in a circle. I knew they were trying to tell me something was going to happen. Half an hour later, Vanessa, my younger daughter, called me all shook up and crying that her car had stopped running in the middle of the road, and she almost got hit. That issue was resolved, and everything was good again. Then about one to two hours later, they were out there again, just circling around and around, and I knew that something else was going to occur, and sure enough, a text came through from my eldest daughter, Priscilla: "Hurry, call the police."

There was a search warrant for her ex-boyfriend, and she knew where he was; she wanted me to call for her. I called the police and gave them the information. I finished out my day at work and went home. The following day, I return to work as usual and a bunch of ravens showed up again; this time, they were not screaming but just hanging out, and I knew it was for a reason because there were so many of them. I called Vanessa to check in on her and told her the ravens were back again and that this meant that something was going to happen again, and to please be safe. Sure enough, two hours later, I received a call from I believe the state's attorney's office that they had apprehended Priscilla's ex-boyfriend. My dad is amazing; the raven is amazing.

Red Lizard

April 18, 2016

My last day of work before my vacation starts tomorrow! I am so excited! I am going to Arizona for the very first time! I am on my lunch break, and as usual, I love to be outside in nature and walk. As I am coming up to the sidewalk, I see a miniature red lizard! It ran so fast across the sidewalk. I have been walking this same route for years and years, and I have never ever seen a miniature lizard ever, and today, I see one! I know that this is a sign and a confirmation that I am going to Arizona tomorrow! Angels are amazing!

Angel on Plane

April 19, 2016

Geo and I are flying out to Arizona today; this is my very first time, and I am so excited. Arizona is the state that I want to live and spend the rest of my life in. I am ready to explore all the beauty that God has created. Vanessa just arrived and is ready to take us to the airport. We take a few photos and off to the airport we go. Once inside the airport, I become even more anxious to get on this plane and start my journey out west. I call everyone and tell them we are close to boarding time, and I love them very much.

The announcement is made; flight to Phoenix Arizona is now boarding. Our number gets called to board the plane; we show our ticket and proceed. As we are walking through the boarding bridge to get to the plane entrance, I can overhear the pilot on the phone speaking to someone on the other end and telling them, "What do you mean, 'Is it serious?' Without the hydraulics, we have no brakes."

This was happening as I was about to enter the plane. I was immediately stopped from boarding the plane, and an announcement was made overhead that because of mechanical issues with this plane, everyone was being routed to another plane. I was so upset because I did not want to wait a minute longer for my dream to begin, but I totally understood why: safety first. We were told to report to another gate, which was clearly on the other end of the airport.

As we exit the boarding bridge, I noticed a very shiny penny on the carpet, and I know that Penelope (my spirit guide) is with me, and this makes me feel better. So here we are about one hundred people all walking to our new gate destination when I noticed one passenger carrying a pet carrier; as I got closer, I noticed there was a cat in that carrier. I love cats. We continue to walk to our gate, and I am hoping that they are also going to be on our flight because of the kitty.

Ahhh, finally we are at our gate and the couple with the cat carrier has also stopped at the same gate, so now I definitely know that the cat will be on our flight too. I quickly tell Geo that we have a cat going with us, and I got to go see the cat while we are waiting to be called to board the plane. I went over to introduce myself and inquired about the cat; they said that their old neighbors moved to Arizona and asked them if they would watch their cat until they got settled in, and they would pay for their trip out there. What a great neighbor! I then asked them what is the cat's name, and they replied, "Angel." Oh my god! My first thought was angels on the plane; we are going to have a safe flight. Angels are amazing! Amen.

Arrived in Phoenix, Arizona, and I am so excited! We pick up our rental, a yellow Volkswagen Beetle and zoomed everywhere until it was time for dinner. I want to remember my first meal here, so I chose Red Lobster. I love their shrimp scampi. The hostess is now ready to seat us, and as we are following her, I noticed a very shiny dime on the blue carpet! I quickly pick it up and turned around to show Geo who is directly behind me. My father is here! My father is here!

I am so excited to know that my father was here to greet me on my *very first day in Arizona*! I love you, Dad, you have my heart. Yes, I took a picture.

Mother's Day: A Vision from Heaven

May 8, 2016

Mother's Day, and every one of my five kids called me but were too busy to stop by and say hello. It kind of saddened me at that moment, and guilt set in. I was thinking to myself was I a bad mother that not one of my kids couldn't even stop and see me? Well, I was not going to let this bring me down! I wanted to take Geo to see the twenty-five-foot tall gold-leafed bronze statue of the Blessed Mother for quite some time now and what better day than today, Mother's Day!

It was a long drive to get there (close to three hours) but well worth it. As we started to approach the area, we could see her; she was a vision of beauty, and I could feel my inner soul at peace. She sits on a ninety-foot tower with her arms wide open at the entrance. We enter the shrine, which is off a mountainside and start walking around; there is so much peace and love in the air, one can feel it. There are religious statues, scriptures written in every direction, small yet gentle waterfalls, and streams. There is even a place to light a candle and send a prayer. Geo is so taken in by all this beauty.

As we continue to walk around and are taking this all in we are also taking pictures. We come up to a mosaic picture of the Blessed Mary and Geo tells me to stand by her and takes a picture. After the picture is taken, I step away and start walking and something tells me to look up. So I look up into the sky, which starts to change in color; it goes from a greenish color to a light blue, and then I see her! I am seeing the Blessed Mother right before my eye. She has on her blue veil and is facing me. What a blessing from heaven to me. My first thought was she was telling me I was a good mother and wishing me a happy Mother's Day. I was so deeply touched and moved by her presence. What a special Mother's Day; this will forever be instilled in my mind and heart. I quickly said a prayer to her. Before we knew it, the announcement was made that the shrine would be closing soon, so we started to walk to the exit, and then we left. Thank you, Blessed Mother Mary, for loving me.

Dime at MVA for Skyler

May 16, 2016

Today is the day Skyler goes for his learner's permit; we are both nervous. We get to the MVA and check in. We then proceed to go take a seat and wait to be called by the next station when we both noticed a dime on the floor where it meets the wall. I am so excited and tell Skyler that my dad is here with us, and I know that he is going to pass. Yes, Skyler ends up passing! My dad is amazing, and I am happy that he is here at this special moment in his grandson's life. Yes, I took a picture.

Penelope

June 6, 2016

Start of the work day when I noticed an image appear on the TV monitor, which resembles my spirit guide, Penelope. I quickly decide to go outside and get a better look to confirm that it is her. Once outside, I can clearly see her silhouette in the water. She has on her long dress that she always wears. She is facing the entrance/exit door to the building and has a halo over her head. I am most sure that this is her; the only thing that is different is that she has a halo for the first time, which causes me to think about it. I take a picture and continue about my work day. It is now 12:41 p.m. and very close to the end of my shift. I am opening up the last few boxes of UPS to receive them into the system when I see the DVD titled *The Confirmation* is in one of the boxes, and I quickly knew I was receiving my confirmation that it was Penelope that I saw early this morning. Penelope is amazing.

Upset about House

June 24, 2016

Received a phone call from Columbia bank regarding my house and what to do with it. I explain my situation, and he gave me options. Robert really screwed me over with this.

"He is not responsible for any payments anymore," says the bank rep. After receiving this phone call, I was upset and almost crying. I couldn't get a hold of anyone to vent so I started speaking with Penelope and asking her to please come through please come through. "I really need to speak to you." I was venting for at least twenty minutes. I also told her I need money just to make everything go back to zero balance everywhere and to help me sell the house. I repeatedly asked her to please speak with me and that I see her everywhere. Well, hours later, I want to stop by China Star to get shrimp fried rice on our way to Geo's poker night at Delaware Park, and when I finished my meal, I opened up my fortune cookie, and this is what it read: "ALL THE TROUBLES YOU HAVE WILL PASS AWAY VERY QUICKLY." In my heart, I knew that Penelope was answering me. I love you, Penelope.

I am sitting outside at Delaware Park, and as I finished writing this, the sun came out. I'm walking up to the casino now, and I'm thinking about God because the sky is so beautiful and so mystical-looking today, and I come across a sign on the back window of a vehicle that reads the following: "PUT YOUR TRUST IN GOD." Thank you, Jesus, thank you, God. I do believe. Yes, I took a picture.

Cody's Guardian Angel

June 26, 2016

Cody was riding his bike from Dunkin' Donuts when he had a seizure. Several people stopped to help him, and one very important person stood out; it was a man that seemed to know a lot about what was going on with Cody. He informed the paramedics of the seizure-like symptoms that Cody was exhibiting, which really helped out the paramedics. He then just disappeared into the crowd. I believe this was Cody's guardian angel helping him out. I found out this later when I went to the hospital. Angels are amazing. Amen.

Penelope Poses

July 1, 2016

As I am looking out my bedroom window, I can see an image of Penelope (my spirit guide) as clear as a cloud could ever be seen. She is so captivating that I cannot stop looking at her. Her beautiful smile, her hair up in a bun, her long dress, knees sort of bent, and she even has her left arm bent behind her head as though she is posing for a picture. She is so beautiful. I am so taken in by her beauty that I am paralyzed at the moment. I then have to capture this moment with a picture. I then quickly head outside to see an even clearer view not obstructed by the screen, and when I look up into the evening sky, I also can see a blue raven appear with its wings spread wide open as the clouds disperse. God is amazing. Yes, I took a picture.

Found a Ten-inch Feather

July 15, 2016

I was outside walking on my lunch break when a car comes nearly inches away from almost clipping me. It could have run me over. I was all shaken up, and I had envisioned myself dismembered all over the road, a very scary thought. I quickly went into prayer and thanked all the angels watching over me, and within a minute and a half, there on the ground, I found a ten-inch feather! The angels heard me. Amen, Lord, amen. I got myself together and decided to call my mother to change my mindset of what just happened. She tells me that a terrorist in a box truck ran over and killed forty-eight people about an hour ago, and it was all over the news. OMG, I almost got hit by a car. I had a vision of my body all dismembered. Did I just predict the future of what my mother was going to tell me? Maybe I'm gonna learn to be a medium or psychic. LOL. After I said that, I found another feather; this one had royal blue in it. God bless the souls of the people who lost their lives in that horrifying accident.

Message from Angel through Radio

July 15, 2016

As I am going to get Chinese food, I ask my angels, Father, and Penelope to send me a message through the radio. I turn the radio on. I hear the following words, "You know it's true. Every little thing I do, I do it for you." This song is by Bryan Adams, and it was the last words that I heard before the song ended, and I knew that my angels had communicated with me. Amen.

I See Christ!

July 18, 2016

Turned on the water to rinse the bottom of my shoes while at work. Then had to re-rinse again, and then a third time when I noticed an image start to show. At first I thought it was an angel. I even looked at it through the television monitor; it was definitely something spiritual. I then went outside, and as I rinsed again, I saw what I believe is a shadow of Jesus Christ. Thank you, angels. Yes, I took a picture.

Flying Penny

July 19, 2016

Driving home on the back roads, halfway home, I asked the angels to ride home with me. As soon as I said this, something came flying into my car. It hit me hard. I thought it might've been a bug, but I could not locate it. About ten minutes later, I felt something move between my legs.

I quickly jumped and placed my hand between my legs. There was a penny there. Penelope (my spirit guide) had stopped in.

"I Need to Change My Life" and Cracked Shield

July 28, 2016

Driving up to Delaware Park again to meet Geo who is playing cards and gambling, I'm not in a great mood. I hate when I feel Geo has the upper hand. I am venting, and I yell out, "I need to change my life." Bang! Something hits my windshields, and CRACK! Angels are listening.

Jesus Christ Our Lord

August 31, 2016

I was going to the gynecologist's office for my little tear, which kept occurring after I had my surgery, and I was referred to see another doctor. I asked the Lord and my angels to be there with me. I went to put gas in my car, and there was a shiny penny, and I knew that Penelope was going to be with me. (She sends me shiny pennies.)

Then as I was walking to the building, there it was! A picture of Jesus Christ our Lord in a newspaper on the pavement facing me; now that was a *big sign*! I knew that the Lord was with me in spirit, and I knew that I was going to be okay. Thank you, Lord. Then as I left the doctor's office, the raven was singing nonstop, and I knew my father was with me. Thank you, Dad. Lastly, as I walked to my car, there was a shiny penny once again. Penelope was telling me she was there from beginning to end. I love you, Penelope, and I believe in you.

Priscilla Found a Dime

September 3, 2016

After Priscilla received a 100 percent on her CNA exam and was walking out of her classroom to head to her car, she found a dime, and she called me. I told her my father was there with her and congratulating her! My dad is amazing.

Happy Birthday, Bill

September 4, 2016

At Hollywood Casino, I had just found out that the dealer's birthday was last week so I told him I would bring in a cake today. On his break, we went outside with a couple of his coworkers to sing "Happy Birthday" to him, cut the cake, and chat. As he started to speak highly about his deceased sister, I saw a bright light to his right, and I knew she was there in spirit. As we were then walking back to go into the casino, I saw a heart-shaped rock. Someone is sending a message of love from above, I showed Geo. Then as we turned the corner to go toward the front door, I saw a matchbook on the sidewalk that read "THANK YOU" on the cover of it, and I knew in my heart it was a message from his sister, thanking me for making her brother's birthday special. Yes, I took a picture.

Angel with Wings

September 5, 2016

We went by the church to watch the summer sunset, and before Geo walked over, I said a little prayer for an angel to appear for me and open up my mind and ears to his word. Then after the sun had set, there appeared an angel with a halo in the sky. Thank you, Penelope; thank you, angels. Yes, I took a picture.

"I Will Never Let You Down"

September 7, 2016

I had an emotional morning with my son Cody. Geo was trying to talk to me about the situation, and it was frustrating me. I told him I was about to reach the top of the volcano and explode! I cannot stand this stress: the house, two younger sons causing heartache, bills, and work! I need a good cry! Geo and Cody are now in the car, both arguing and yelling. We dropped Cody off, and later, we picked him back up. I was crying, still stressing. We to go to Bertucci's and had a quiet meal. I cried a little more because Cody would not shake Geo's hand when Geo offered to forgive and forget. I am so helpless, sad, and my heart is broken. As we finished up, I left Geo and Cody to go wash my hands. I was the only one in the bathroom, and as I placed the used paper towel on the counter, it formed the shape of an angel, and then I heard it! On the radio above my head, I kept hearing the song on the radio saying, "I will never let you down. I will never let you down." And I knew my angels are 100 percent there for me.

Found a Penny

September 8, 2016

Leaving Delaware Park Casino, Geo is playing poker there, and I was walking to his car to go get Chinese food when I received a call from Cody's phone. It was Josh, his friend; he said that Cody had suffered a seizure, and the ambulance was there. As I was hearing the events that lead to the seizure, I was almost to the car when I noticed a shiny penny under Geo's car, and I knew that Cody was going to be all right. Penelope (my spirit guide) drove down with me as I prayed for my son, as I drove very fast to get to the hospital. Yes, I took a picture. Angels are amazing. Thank you, Penelope.

Raven at Dentist Office

September 9, 2016

Skyler is having his wisdom teeth pulled out today, and I went outside to call for a follow-up visit for Cody after his seizure episode, and as I was on the phone with the doctor's office, a black raven showed up. He stayed there the whole time until the appointment was set and confirmed, and then he flew away. He is also here to acknowledge that he knows that Skyler's getting his wisdom teeth pulled. I love you, Dad. Thank you for being here with me and for supporting me; thank you for sending the raven.

Homeless Angel

September 23, 2016

After dropping off Geo at Delaware Park, I went to Walgreen's. As I was parking, I could hear this beautiful sound of music, but I could not tell where it was coming from. Was it playing in the distance, or a radio station outside? All I know was that it was so good. As I turned to see where it was coming from, I noticed a man with a guitar sitting on the sidewalk next to Walgreen's, singing and playing. He was so good. I got all of Geo's loose change out of his car and placed it in his guitar case, and I began talking to him. I loved our conversation. We talked about how he became homeless and how he survives out in the world. I told him about my dream of changing the world and taking every homeless person off the streets. I asked for any advice and he offered the following: place to sleep, wash clothes, store personnel belongings, and training for learning a trade. He also said, "I would need a doctor, nurse, and security on call and a lawyer to draw up all the paperwork." This man's name is Harry, and he is a carpenter. He is fifty-two and has one daughter, twenty-one, whom he adores. I told him what my ex-husband told me that if he was homeless, he would get a one-way ticket to Florida where its warm all the time, and Harry's response was that he was heading to North Carolina. The same place we are going to next week! Is this a sign? Wow!

I asked him if I could take a picture with him, and he said yes. So I squatted down next to him and pointed the camera toward us and took a picture. After the picture was taken, I went to get up, and there I noticed an angel sitting next to him, so I told him and he told me they always are. He said that he feels as though God has a purpose for him as I believe that he has a purpose for me. I am so grateful that the Lord has brought me to this man. Thank you, Lord. I learned so much from this wonderful man today. As I got into the car and about to drive off, I noticed jar of peanuts in the back seat. I called him over and gave them to him. Thank you, Lord, for this experience. As I drove off, I pulled up to a red light, and I waited for it to turn green, when a school bus pulled up next to me with two words on the side of it which read "FIRST STUDENT" in capital letters, and it quickly reminded me of the reading with Ray from Sedona, Arizona, which he said that I am a healer, I am a teacher, and before we are teachers, we are students. This was my first lesson learned from a homeless person. Thank you, Lord. Thank you, angels, for this experience. Amen.

$20/$20

September 23, 2016

When I entered Walgreen's, I wanted to get Harry (homeless man) a T-shirt because he said that he had been wearing the same shirt for five days. There were no T-shirts, only hooded sweaters, and they were too expensive for me, and besides, he had a flannel shirt in his knapsack so I asked God to let me find a $20 so that I could give it him. Never found a $20 that day in there.

When I arrived at Delaware Park, there was a white piece paper on the ground next to a car, so I picked it up and it read, "202." Well, today, we stopped by the gas station on the way the casino, and Geo asked me to give him four numbers so I gave him 2020, the number that I saw on the white paper the day before, and he said, "Really?"

I said, "Yes, unless you want to play 202."

Well, later, when we arrived at Delaware Park I was walking way ahead of Geo, and I saw money on the ground. I walked over to it and picked it up and it was two $20 bills! So I know that I am supposed to give Harry a $20 when I see him again. Thank you, Lord.

Dirt Angel

October 25, 2016

Geo and I were taking care of Vanessa's cat while Vanessa was pregnant. And you know cats, they love plants; they eat them, smell them, use them to relieve themselves, and even kill them. As I came into the living room, I noticed that the cat had gotten into one of my large plants and had gotten dirt all over the light-cream-colored rug. At first sight, I was upset with the cat. I went to get the vacuum to clean it up, and when I returned, I noticed that the dirt resembled a child angel with wing. It was unexplainable; angels are amazing. Yes, I took a picture.

And a Rainbow Appeared

November 29, 2016

As I awoke today, it rained. It rained all day. Today I received news that the appraisal for my house was higher than what the buyer had offered, which caused the proposal to be denied, and my house now will go to auction on December 14 (my daughter's birthday, of all days). I lost the battle today. I was sad, but life goes on, and everything is for a reason.

Toward the end of my workday, I was a little emotional because of it. I wept for a minute, and then the day was over. As a walked to my car, soft rain hit my face. I got into my car and started my journey home. As I drove home, I felt the urge to pray, so I started to pray to the Lord and telling him of all my faults and failures and all that I wanted to accomplish and be and that I needed his help.

I gave my prayers up to the Lord, and as I was driving home, I looked over to my left, and I could see the gray sky opening up to a beautiful clear blue sky only for a moment. Still in prayer, I could see the sun was trying to shine as the soft rain continued to gently come down as a watched from the rearview mirror the streets shined like diamonds. It was so incredibly beautiful and endless, and then I saw it, a *rainbow*, and I knew that the Lord had listened to my prayers. Tears came down my face as I pulled over to take a picture of the beautiful sight. I'm at peace, Lord. I love you, Lord. Thank you, my Lord.

Found $5 on Priscilla's Birthday

December 14, 2016

Today is Priscilla's birthday, and I don't have the funds to take her out to dinner like I like to do every year, so in prayer this morning, I prayed for the gift of a $100 find so that I can take her out to dinner. On my lunch break as usual, I like to walk, and today was a very, very highly windy day. As I walked past the bank, there in the bushes I see a $5 bill! Now I have passed this bank hundreds of times over the many years of walking there, and I have never found a single dollar, so I know it's a sign from my angels. Angels are amazing.

You Are Blessed

December 16, 2016

Went to Kohl's with Geo to pick out a new dress for the casino, and as we were looking at the clothing, I accidentally knocked over a display of boxed jewelry, so I squatted to start picking them up, and as I began to pick up each box and place them on the table, I noticed that there was an extra pair of hands helping me. It was a very young man. He was helping me put the boxes back on the table. Then with the last box, he handed it to me saying, "This one is missing its base," so I looked at it and it read "YOU ARE BLESSED," and yes, I knew it was a sign from above for me. Angels are amazing. Yes, I took a picture.

Priscilla's Food Stamps

December 21, 2016

Priscilla found a dime! Priscilla was at the department of human resources because they shortage her funds to feed her and her children. My father was with her to ensure she got what she was entitled to, and she did. I love you, Dad, thank you for watching over my children. Yes, she took a picture.

Christmas White Flower

December 25, 2016

I have a lemon tree that I bought a few years ago, and it blooms whenever it wishes to. I noticed a few weeks ago it was getting buds, and I thought that on my birthday, I would get a message from my father, but December 11 came and went and with no flower. :(

Christmas Day: Wow, I had a beautiful white flower open up, and I knew it was a message from my father. I love you, Dad. Buon Natale.

Towel for Sale

January 6, 2017

Geo was asking me to check to see if there were any sales on bath towels while we were at Kohl's yesterday. There were none. So while at work today, I needed to count perfume, which was in the seasonal aisle. We have more than one seasonal aisle, so I had to find the one that had the perfume display in it. As I walked around, I noticed there were towels marked down, so I took several pictures to show Geo if he liked them. Fifteen hours later, I am looking at all the pictures that I took for the day; at first glance I can clearly see a heart on the right-hand corner of the towel, a sign that I am loved. And then I noticed an even bigger sign on the left side of the towel; I could see the Virgin Mary. She is again in her blue veil. I know this definitely is a sign from above. Thank you, angels. Yes, I took a picture.

Angel Acid Stain Again

January 17, 2017

I went over to place new checklists on all the forklifts when I noticed an acid spill that resembled a male angel. I first noticed the stain earlier this morning but did not see the whole angel because it was covered with debris, but I knew it was going to be a sign for me; the angel was darker in color versus the female acid angel that has been there for a few years earlier. Yes, I took a picture; angels are everywhere.

College Dime

January 20, 2017

I went to college to register for my class on SPIRITS AND GUIDES, a gift from my mother, and as we were walking back to the car, I found a dime. I knew my father was with me and approved of what I was doing. I love you, Dad. Yes, I took a picture.

Found Dime

February 3, 2017

Geo, Priscilla, Skyler, Conner, Bentley, and I went to Texas Roadhouse for dinner my treat. When it was time to pay, my Capital One card was declined, even though I just paid it this morning at 6:00 a.m. total of $232. Geo then said, "I told you this was going to happen." I then quickly pulled out my APG card and hoped for the best, and yes, it was approved. As soon as I went to get up there, it was a dime! I knew her father was here, and he would not let me down. Thank you, Dad, I love you. Yes, I took a picture.

Skyler Finds a Dime

February 10, 2017

Yesterday, Skyler was upset about not having a car. As he walked outside of his apartment building, he found a dime. He took a picture and sent it to me. My father is there for him.

A Bouquet of Ravens

February 14, 2017

Today is Valentine's Day! One of my managers received flowers through UPS, and I thought of myself when I used to receive flowers on Valentine's Day, and as soon as I thought about that, the voice of a raven outside the bay door could be heard. I have not seen a raven at work in almost one year now. I quickly went over and opened the door, and there they were between seven and nine ravens all sitting on the railing, and when I opened the door, they all flew up in the air like a bouquet of flowers, and they were going in all different directions. I knew it was a sign from my father sending me Valentine wishes. I love you, Dad, thank you.

Angel in Cemetery

March 21, 2017

I decided to go see my father today because I was having such a spiritual day. As I entered the cemetery, I saw an angel! A female angel. I started to shake; it was so eye-captivating that I had to *stop* and turn my car around to get a closer look. I parked my car and walked up to the angel, so beautiful. I touched it and kneeled before it, and I prayed to her. Thank you for such a visual blessing, Lord. Yes, I took a picture. Amen.

Two Dimes

March 30, 2017

Priscilla was in an accident last night, and today, I went to the police station to get the release report on the car, and as soon as I walked up to the window, there they were two dimes sitting on the windowsill. Thank you, Dad, for being there for me always. I love you. Yes, I took a picture.

Blessed Mary   Entenmann's Cake

April 8, 2017

Went to Redner's grocery store to get iced coffee and a few other items when I saw an Entenmann's fudge cake—yummy. I put it in my cart, and I took a picture of it to send to Geo to see if he wanted it or not, and he declined. So I put the cake back. Later that evening, when I was going through my pictures of the day, I noticed an image on the film of the cake box, so I zoomed in on it, and I saw an image of the Blessed Mary, mother of Jesus! She again had her veil on her head, and I could feel a sense of peace coming over me. Angels are amazing. Amen.

Penny in the Gelato Case at AC

April 19, 2017

We were in Atlantic City. We just left the pool, and Geo wanted to get gelato. As we approached the counter, I saw a dark penny on the floor, and I thought to myself, *It's not Penelope.* Penelope sends me shiny pennies, and as I think this, I looked at the gelato case because I want Geo to sample the caramel flavor, even though he already wants the chocolate flavor. As I looked at the flavor above the chocolate, I see it! A shiny penny! The penny was in the gelato! OMG! I wish I had my camera! Geo and the young lady behind the counter are my witnesses! I told her there was a penny in the gelato, and she took a spoon and got it out then put the tray back into the glass case. See, I can communicate with my angels! I just can't hear them yet. I love you, Penelope.

Learning from My Mistakes

April 20, 2017

At the lawyer's office, waiting to sign on the dotted line, my bank-ruptcy paperwork. All I kept saying to myself is, *I am getting a new start, and I will never buy a house with another person again!* As I kept repeating this over in my head, I opened up the magazine that was next to me on the end table in the waiting room, and it opened up to a page that was titled "Learning from my mistakes." Thank you, angels. Keep guiding me. Yes, I took a picture.

Very Large Snapping Turtle

April 28, 2017

In my prayers this morning, I asked to receive a sign from my father and my other angels. Then again, when I went on my fifteen-minute break, I asked my father again. Then lunchtime came, and I asked again for a big sign from my father. As I was walking back from my walk, I noticed that this one van that normally blocks the area that I would like to walk on was not blocking that section, so I decided I was going to walk in that area.

I was walking through the car dealership, and in there they have over two hundred cars lined up side by side, and I decided to cross over at the same exact location that there is a large snapping turtle in between the cars. Growing up, my dad would always catch large snapping turtles like this one. Oh my god, that is 110 percent a sign from my father that I asked for. There is no other way to explain it. Everything had to line up perfectly for this situation to happen. A black raven then flies right above me, another confirmation. Yes, I took a picture, and yes, I went to the cemetery. I wanted to thank my father personally. I love you, Dad, with all my heart.

Black Angel

May 15, 2017

I was walking on my fifteen-minute break when I noticed in the tall grass there was a black trash bag in the shape of a human, and for a minute, I thought to myself, *I hope there's not a dead body under it*, so I had to take a closer look. As I approached the bag, I noticed that it resembled an angel with wings. I could also see the side view of a face. Is this a sign for me?

Yes, I took a picture. This angel remained out there for weeks to come.

Raven Flaps Its Wings at Me

May 31, 2017

I was going to my bankruptcy hearing today to finally END the 707 chapter of my life with Robert completely! As I'm about to enter the Fort McHenry tunnel, there sitting on a ledge was a raven that I almost missed, *but* because it lifted off the ledge about two feet high and flapped its wings back and forth, back and forth, it got my attention. It was like the raven was clapping for me. I definitely knew it was a sign from my father and that everything was gonna be fine, thank you, Dad, I love you. You are always there for me.

Eye Watching

June 5, 2017

We had an appointment with the eye doctor to see if the shingles virus had gotten into Geo's eyeball, which could leave him blind. As I was working, I noticed an eyeball sticker suck on the floor right next to my work area. I didn't think anything else about it, but I kept passing by it and just wondering if I should take a picture of it or not, and if it was a sign. Well, it wasn't until I was driving home that it hit me. It was a sign from my angels, reminding me of Geo's eye and his appointment. I immediately called one of my coworker and asked them if they would take a picture and send it to me because I was not sure if it would still be there the next day, and I was right; it wasn't. Thank you, angels.

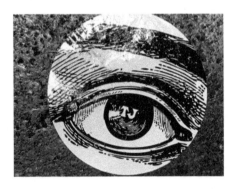

Notary for Mom

June 6, 2017

Every year, my mother receives a notice from the Italian government, asking for proof that she is still living to continue to receive her pension. She fills it out, and we take it to a notary where all they have to do is read it, notarized with a seal, and put their signature on it, and every year it seems like a problem.

The letter is self-explanatory and is also translated in English. The woman at the bank that my mother banks at refused to notarize it, giving us some excuse and her manager backed her up. My mother was *hot*! We left, and we went to the post office where they told us they could not do it neither. My mother was so mad at this point. I told her to calm down and lets go to my bank, M&T. We went into the bank, and within minutes, my mother's letter was read, notarized, and signed. Great customer service!

My mother was happy again. Once everything was finished, one of the bank specialist, Rhonda, saw me and came over to say hello. Again, great customer service. Her nephew had recently passed, and since we are both into the spiritual world, we started to talk about the spirit world and if she has gotten any signs that he crossed over, and I mentioned the dime. I tell her of all the dimes I have received from my father throughout the years. As we were talking about dimes, the lady that notarized my mother's letter said, "That's funny you are talking about dimes because there's a dime under my desk." We all stopped and looked under her desk, and sure enough, there was a dime! Wow, four of us witnessed this. My father is with us, and he helped my mother get her letter notarized. I took the dime, and when we got out to the car, I took a picture of the dime with my mother. My father is amazing! Angels are amazing!

Penelope Appears

June 15, 2017

I am watering my vegetable garden and admiring the beauty of each plant. God had created everything we need here on planet Earth. It is such a relaxing feeling. It is a sunny day, peaceful and quiet. As I finished watering all my plants, I started to put the hose away, and when I was finished, I turned around, and there it was—Penelope's silhouette. Beautiful. Yes, I took a picture.

Found a Canadian Dime!

July 12, 2017

Geo took me to Canada for six days of relaxation and to take in all the views, shops, restaurants that Canada had to offer and of course the breathtaking views of Niagara Falls. I was so excited, I told him it would also be a fun tradition to get a tattoo in every state that we visited, so when people asked about his tattoos, he could tell them that each tattoo was done in a different state, and we were in Canada, so we should look at tattoo parlors in the area for him.

Well, on our last day in Canada, Geo and I were finally heading to a tattoo parlor. We parked in a general parking area and began to walk toward the shop when something shiny next to one of the other cars in the lot caught my eye. As I walked toward it, I noticed it was a dime, a Canadian dime! I was so happy because the whole trip I did not find one dime. I knew being in Canada, it would be hard to find an American dime, but my father found a way to come through! I love you, Dad! Yes, I took a picture.

"Don't Need Material Things"

August 12, 2017

Went to see the statue of the Blessed Mary. While in prayer, a bird sang the whole time. When I went to leave to go to the car for a minute, the bird stopped singing. When I returned to the statue to continue to pray, the bird once again sang. I then finished my prayers, took a few pictures, and left. As I was driving home, I heard the Blessed Mother Mary talking to me in my thoughts. She said I don't need material things: "Be basic, you can't take it with you."

Christmas Tree

December 8, 2017

Got my first check! Only had $2 in my account. Put the check in and thought I would have to wait until Monday to have the available funds because I did not have enough money to cover the check, but the teller surprised me and put it in as cash, so I was then able to use the funds right away. We went to Home Depot to get a tree. I fell in love with the first one I saw. Geo was happy. The tree was a little steep in price, but I did not want a short, five- to six-foot tree. The tree was $45. As Geo went to get the car, I looked down and there I saw an angel, and I knew it was a confirmation that I was supposed to get this tree. At the register, it rang up $32.98! Thank you, angels.

Borrowed Car

December 29, 2017

I had borrowed Julie's car for the week because my car was totaled when it was T-boned in an accident. I told her I was going to give her $20 a day, plus fill her tank up. I was very low on cash, but Friday was payday. Well, on Friday I net $0 and I had her car until Saturday. I net $0 because when I returned to work that week from my ongoing medical issues I had sustained from my car accident, they took out all the back pay from my weekly deductions and taxes, which left me with nothing. I did not know they were going to leave me with nothing; how am I going to pay Julie now and have money for the next week? So I prayed on it. Well, on Saturday, one of my coworkers who I always help out, handed me ten $5 bills; she said it was for me (birthday, Christmas gift), and I was able to pay Julie. Power of prayer is amazing. Angels are amazing. Thank you, angels.

Angel Image

January 4, 2018

First sign of the new year. I am at work and not feeling well because of my concussion symptoms. As I look out on the TV monitor from the receiving office, I could see an angel image on the snow. I take a picture then go outside to get a closer look. It's an angel. I could tell it's a female angel, and she's watching over me; she's beautiful. Thank you, angel.

MRI of the Brain

January 19, 2018

I went to advanced radiology to have my MRI of the brain and neck, again because of the car accident that occurred in October. As I was checking in, I saw it a dime! It was on a yellow Post-it note on the counter next to the computer. I quickly knew my father was with me. I asked the lady behind the counter if I could have the dime, and I would give her a quarter in return. She was happy to give to me but declined the exchange. I asked her why it was there, and she said a patient found it on the floor. I knew it was meant for me.

Fly at Funeral

January 27, 2018

A poker friend of ours suddenly passed away from a heart attack. I was crushed at hearing the news, and I wanted to pay my respects. His name was John Nelson, and in prayer and throughout the days that followed, I asked him for a sign that he had crossed over.

Saturday was his funeral, and an ex-coworker of mine wanted to attend also. As we were listening to the priest, I reminded John in prayer that I wanted a visual sign from him. John was cremated, and his urn was on a little table sitting in front of his picture and flowers all around him. As the memorial mass was being said, a fly caught my eye because it was on the picture of John. The fly was on his face, and then it flew over to a white mum and then disappeared. There are no flies in the wintertime.

So I asked him, "Is this the sign, John?" Moments later, as the priest is holding the cup of wine and saying a prayer over it, the fly lands on the cup and the priest gently moves his hand to the side of the cup to move the fly away. Hopefully, no one noticed. As mass is now ending, I noticed a black object twice the size on the table where the urn is, and it is not moving at all, and people are approaching the table and taking the flowers and roses. I questioned myself and say, *Is that the fly?*

As we all know, a fly will fly away as soon as something comes close to it. My ex-coworker and I started walking up to the table, and I told her that John had given me a sign that he had crossed over. I asked her if she had seen the fly while the memorial was in session, and she named all the places that I had also seen it land. As we approached the table, I noticed it was the fly, and I leaned over to touch it, and yes, the fly let me touch it, and I knew it was a sign from John that he had crossed over. I then took out my phone and videotaped the fly, and it let me touch it for a few seconds and then flew away.

We then head out to the car, and we are fighting the heavy winds that are blowing everything around. We are recapping what just had happened, and as we got into the car, my ex-coworker who had a rose in her hand extended her arm across and pointed to the windshield right in front of me, and there was a fly! Thank you, John. I love you.

Heart-Shaped Sunlight

February 5, 2018

A ray of sunlight was coming through the kitchen window and landed on the floor; it was in a shape of a heart. I looked at the window to see where it was coming from but could not see or explain it, and I knew that it was from above and that I am loved. That day Geo was being mean and ignoring me. Every single time, 100 percent that things are not good between us I always receive a sign of love and support from above. Thank you, Dad; thank you, angels.

Sign of the Cross

February 12, 2018

After putting a pallet of water in the steel, I must have not pulled out my forks all the way out and started to descend them when I heard a crackling noise of wood splitting as my forks were coming down, and then in *slow motion*, the wood started to break off and forming a cross. At first I thought about death. Was I going to die? I then thought to myself a cross is not always a symbol of death. It can also be a positive sign. Yes, I took a picture. Two days later, I had to go to the emergency room because I was hemorrhaging so bad from my menstrual cycle. My angels had prepared me two days earlier so I would not be afraid. Angels are amazing.

Found a Dime

February 24, 2018

I have not seen dime in a long time. I went to Chopsticks to pick up dinner for Geo, and it turned out to be over an hour. I helped a stranger, and then Cody called me and said he had a headache and needed a ride home, so I picked him up from his friend's house, took him to Wawa for dinner, and dropped him back at his friend's house because he was feeling better. I even got a can of cat food for Roscoe.

I was then driving back to Chopsticks while talking and trying to help to Julie about her relationship with my son, Skyler. As I stepped out of the car and walked a few steps, there was a dime right in front of Chopsticks. I went back to my car get the camera, and as I was taking the picture, a man jokingly behind me said, "Oh, I found a dime." Hahaha! He made me smile. I love you, Dad, thank you for being in my life and coming to visit me this evening.

Found a Dime

March 5, 2018

At work and not feeling good. These symptoms from the concussion are taking forever to heal. I want to leave work now, but I'm sort of stuck. I am the only one here. As I walk over to bay door no. 1 there it is, a dime. I know that my father is with me. Yes, I took a picture.

Angel in the Sky

March 15, 2018

Today I bought a brand-new car! As I was signing paperwork, Paul from Florida sent me an angel picture that a friend sent him. I do not know if it was real or not because it was too perfect, but it was a positive sign for me today. Angels are telling me I am heading in the right direction. Yes, I have the picture.

Three Little Birds

March 26, 2018

I was at work doing my daily counts, and I was worrying about everything in my life when the song "Three Little Birds" came on by Bob Marley. The angels were talking to me through the lyrics. "Don't worry about a thing 'cause everything is going to be all right." I was so amazed and blessed and comforted by his words. It made me feel relaxed, and I stopped worrying. I had never heard that song before in my life, but that day, it was meant for me to hear. Angels, I am so blessed that you are in my life. Thank you. Yes, I took a picture of the Sirius radio, which shows the artist and the title of the song.

Jesus Praying

April 5, 2018

I just left Giant from picking up flowers for Mrs. Ficca who was in hospice. As I was leaving the parking lot, I quickly noticed a fresh cut limp that left a bright yellow glow that caught my eye. I saw Jesus with his hands in prayer with a bird over his head. I knew it was a sign that Jesus was praying over Mrs. Ficca with us. I wanted to spend as much time with her as possible so I returned the next day to take a picture.

Speeding Feather

April 9, 2018

I was leaving the funeral home after paying my respects to a beautiful Italian woman and friend, Mrs. Ficca. As I walked around the front of the building to find my parked car, a raven flew by my path, singing, and I knew my father had visited.

I got into my car and drove around to the exit, but I did not know which way to turn, left or right, so I pulled in forward in a parking spot to Google my way home, when a car pulled up right behind me. I signaled the car to go around, but the car would not move, so I stepped out of the car and walked over to the car to tell the person that I was in a parking spot, not on the road, and she apologized. I said that's okay, and I turned and pointed to where the exit to the road began, and when I looked forward, I saw a black object twirling straight down and landed right in front of my car. I quickly turned around and said to the girl in the vehicle, "DID YOU SEE THAT!" and she said no. I said, "That object that was coming out of the sky!" She said no again. So I walked over to the front of my car, and there it was, two feathers! One was large, and one was very small, and I knew it was sign from heaven and Mrs. Ficca. Yes, I took a picture.

Raven on Truck

April 10, 2018

I was heading to a viewing of another very special lady who always reminded me of Marylin Monroe. She was always very kind and nice to me. My mother and father once had a discussion about a month before he passed away about heaven and whoever passed away first would tell the other how heaven was. You have to be open to receive spirit; if you're not open, you will not receive the message, and apparently my mother was not open to see or hear the message.

So my father told Rosa Lipera (Marylin Monroe) in a dream that heaven was beautiful; it was more beautiful than he had imaged. Rosa Lipera then called my mother and told her of the dream. My father had once again communicated from heaven. This is the woman I was going to pay my respects to this evening. I had told my father in prayer as I was driving down Interstate 95 that I wanted him to be with me at the viewing and to give me a sign that he would be there. Within ten seconds of me saying this, I looked to my right as a tractor trailer was passing me, and I saw a raven drawn on its back door with the word "RAVEN" written right next to it. I knew that was a sign from my father 100 percent and that he would be with me at the viewing. Yes, I took a picture. I love you, Dad.

Found a Dime

April 11, 2018

I wanted a Bertucci's pizza; I was craving it. I had gotten the same order the day I went to the viewing for Mrs. Ficca. When I had come out, I found a dime right next to the curb; there were no cars around, and I did not see it in on the way in. I knew it was a sign from above. Thank you, Dad, and Mrs. Ficca. Yes, I took a picture.

Found a Dime

April 18, 2018

I took my two grandsons Conner and Bentley to Giant with me to get dinner, and I was worrying about money. Every time I worry about my financial state, I receive a dime from my father, and I can relax knowing that he is saying it's okay get the groceries and feed your grandchildren. I saw the dime by my car, and there were no other cars anywhere near my car when we went in. Yes, I took a picture with Conner in it. Thank you, Dad.

Raven at Work

April 23, 2018

I was taking a break outside when I saw a water stain that resembled a raven, and I knew it was a message from my father. Yes, I took a picture.

We Got You Covered

May 2, 2018

Left work early because of a doctor appointment today in Delaware for my ongoing concussion. As I was driving to the 795 light, I was in prayer. A friend of mine from Delaware is in Arizona visiting his ill mother, and I wanted to say an extra prayer for her, and then I said an extra prayer for myself, and then as I was finishing up my prayers, I looked up, and I see a sign written on the side of a van that says "YOU ARE COVERED" in American slang that means that someone has my back, and it will be taken care of. Thank you, angels. I love you. Yes, I took a picture.

Be Your Own Boss

May 10, 2018

I was praying yesterday and again today that I wanted to be my own boss. I wanted to set my own rules, work my own hours, and be in control of life. Well, today, we were watching the movie *Coneheads* when the character of Otto played by Sinbad said there are three rules to being successful: "Be your own boss." I knew right away it was a sign from my angels to me. They were answering my prayers. Thank you, angels. I love you.

Let's Drive

May 18, 2018

Today, I scheduled my son, Cody for his driving classes. I had to do it. I love my son, and I want him to have everything I could give him and the freedom to drive and to go anywhere you want is a gift. I know it will make him very happy when he can get in a car and drive away instead of being stuck somewhere he doesn't want to be or feeling sad and blue. It's expensive, and I live paycheck to paycheck. I paid half the balance to get him in, and the remainder I will pay in a couple of weeks. As I came out of the shower and was getting ready, I went over to the window to look out; at the same time, a white car drove around the court and then quickly drove out. On the car door it read, "LET'S DRIVE" in blue letters, and I knew that was a sign for me that I did the right thing. Amen.

Don't Stop Believing

May 31, 2018

Woke up at 3:00 a.m. to get ready for work and looked into my bank account to see if my car payment was taken out. It had been five days. Well, to my surprise, my doctor's office took out $100, which they were not supposed to until Friday. I was so mad! Now my car payment was going to be $100 short, and when they would go to pull it out, it would charge me $38 insufficient funds. I could not do anything until 9:00 a.m. everything was closed. I got ready and left for work. I was still so upset that I could not go into prayer mode, so I decided to turn on the radio to change the tone, and when I did, the song on the radio was "Don't Stop Believing" by Journey. It was written on my car screen, and at seeing that, it totally changed my demeanor from a negative feeling to a very positive feeling, which lasted all day long! Thank you, angels.

Fortune Cookie Message

June 15, 2018

Still tense feeling between Geo and I, went to Chopsticks for dinner, and after dinner, I read my fortune cookie. The message read, "Domestic conditions demand your attention." Geo was literally knocked out a few days earlier in a random act of violence, an incident that occurred at the casino and the male suspect got away. Yes, I took a picture. Angels are amazing.

Heart in the Sky with Arrow

June 26, 2018

Relationship still is in the negative. I want a change. I want to be happy. I walked outside, and there in the sky I see a heart with an arrow going through it. Thank you, angels. I love you and thank you for being there for me. Yes, I took a picture.

"Never Give Up"

July 3, 2018

I was a little heartbroken this afternoon because of Geo saying we are only sex partners a couple of days ago. He had been really nice in person the last two days, but we don't talk anymore during the day when we are away from each other. I know that he is painting, but he does get a break at least a lunch break. I also thought of a lot of negative things that he has done to me in our relationship in the last five and a half years, and coming to grips with it now, maybe we really don't love each other even though he told me he loves me today.

I was emotional today around him, and I've had a few tears. We went to Kohl's to get him an outfit for a wedding that we are invited to this Thursday. As I was waiting for him outside the dressing room, I saw a shirt that read, "NEVER GIVE UP" with two red boxing gloves pictured. I knew this was a message from my angels. I'm a little confused, though, is it not to give up on this relationship, or is it too not give up on life, keep going. These are the moments that I wish I had more clarity so I can fully understand the message. I was grateful that I received a message from spirit.

Heart and Nana

July 3, 2018

I was on my lunch break and arguing with my mother over the phone; she is always so negative about me wanting to move out west when I received a sign from above to love my mother. It was three pink hearts and the word *Nana* written in sidewalk chalk. One of my mother's very favorite colors is pink, and I always associate it with her and my kids call her Nona (grandmother in Italian); in America they say *nana*. The message I was receiving through spirit world was to love your mother, so I quickly changed my demeanor and started calming down. I do love my mother, and I only get one mother; she is seventy-eight years old. Yes, I took a picture. Thank you, angels.

Found a Dime

July 4, 2018

I was deep in thought about my relationship and my future with Geo while I was at work this morning, and at around 5:20 a.m., I looked down on the ground and there was a dime, and I knew my father was with me. And in my thoughts, I knew he was telling me that if I need him, he will always be there for me. Thank you, Dad.

Found a Dime in New York City

July 4, 2018

We are in New York City; we have a wedding to go to tomorrow. As I was praying for the souls that perished in the 9/11 attacks as I stand in front of the buildings, I find a dime. Earlier today, I had asked my father to come with me to the wedding, and yes, he is here with me. God bless you, Dad. I love you.

Angel in the Sky of New York City

July 4, 2018

I wanted to arrive a day earlier for a wedding we were invited to in New York City and watch the fireworks here. As we are walking around and thinking about the 9/11 incident that happened sixteen years ago, I see an angel appear above the sky as big as day, and I know this area has been blessed forever. Yes, I took a picture. God bless all the angels and all the souls that went to heaven on that day.

Prayer with Jesus

August 2, 2018

I started on my three-mile walk, and ten minutes into it, it started to rain. I didn't know if it was going to last or not but didn't want to chance it, so I cut through the backyard, and as soon as I was about to enter the garage, it started pouring down!

I decided to sit down on my aunt Zia Lina's sofa, which she gave me, and I got the urge to pray. As I sat down, I looked up right at the portrait of Jesus that was on the mantle, and I decided to get up and get the picture and place it on the red chair facing me so I could pray to Jesus face-to-face. I prayed and spoke to him at the same time. I was also crying so much, and I do not know why.

Sometimes I couldn't even look at him, and I do not know why. It was tranquil and very quiet in the home. It was just Jesus and me. I prayed and also told him what I wanted out of life for myself and my children. As my prayer ended, I wished for a rainbow for confirmation that my prayer was heard since it was raining. A couple of hours later, the sun came out at the same time it was raining, so I went to the backyard to see if a rainbow was present but did not see one, but I definitely know there was one out there. I love you, Jesus.

Man with No Limbs

August 4, 2018

For the last few weeks I have been having issues with both my arms; they are both serious. I feel such pain, and I cannot do the things that I want to do because of my pain level and range of motion. I feel useless at times; it's sad. Geo has actually said to me something to the fact that at least "You have your arms." Well, last evening while at Delaware Park Casino, I noticed a man walk up to the bar alone and sit down. He had no hands or feet. As I sat in my seat, I felt an urge…

This urge was that I had to speak to this man. Well, I am told I am an earth angel so I got an excuse, and I sat right next to him. We starting talking, and we talked for hours while Geo played poker; we even went downstairs to listen to the band play. We then went outside and sat on the bench and talked some more. In that time, I had realized why I had met this man. It was a sign from the angels. I have my arms, I should be grateful, and when I think I got it bad, and I am complaining about both my arms, there is someone far off worse than me, and I should not complain. I am grateful that I met this wonderful man. Angels are amazing.

Found a White Feather

August 7, 2018

We were at Delaware Park, and the man that I met with no limbs on Saturday was here. I had told him that we were going to be there on Tuesday night because it was a fun night to play poker because of the fun people that come out on Tuesday nights. As I was sitting next to him, the dealer asked me if I wouldn't mind helping this man by showing him each of his hands that were dealt to him. I said okay. So for the next thirty-five minutes, I was helping this wonderful man with his cards. This man was really playing well. Well, soon, it happened Geo went all in and was knocked out, so we had to leave, and as we walked over to my car, there it was, a feather—a white feather! I automatically knew it was a sign from above. Angels were happy. Yes, I took a picture.

I'll Keep Holding On

August 10, 2018

I called Barnes and Noble to see if *The Secret* was available on audio (CD), and the woman on the other end asked, "By Rhonda Byrne?" and I replied, "Yes," so she checked and said, "Yes, we have one copy on hand, I will put it on hold for you."

I quickly replied, "Hold on, how much is it?"

She replied, "Twenty-four dollars."

OMG, I was thinking to myself, *too much!* I asked her to check to see if they really have it since it is only calling for one. She places me on hold, and as I am on hold, I'm thinking, *Should I hang up? Should I hang up?* and while I'm thinking this, I hear this annoying song playing over and over and over…

"I'll keep holding on, I'll keep holding on, I'll keep holding on," and then I get it! It's a sign! It's a sign from the angels! I am supposed to get this audio (CD). She came back on the phone and said, "Yes, we have it." She then asked for my name to hold it, and I thanked her for helping me and I went to get it. I had to tell the lady on the phone, and Terry (the best physic/medium ever and a great friend who always believes in me) what just happened! She replied, "That's how they work." Angels are amazing. The song is called "I'll Keep Holding On" by Simply Red.

Found a Dime

August 18, 2018

Geo asked to borrow $260 for the poker tournament. I was a little hesitant because I did not know if he was going to pay me back right away, and I had car insurance due, and I was still $31 short. Well, to make a short story, Geo cashed tonight $459! I went to cash his poker chips and then proceeded to head back to the table, and there in my pathway was a dime. I was so happy and knew my father was here. I gave Geo the cash, and he repaid me $300. In my heart, I knew my father was there to help Geo win the tournament so that he could repay me back, and I even got the $31 that I was short to pay my bill. Thank you, Dad, for loving me.

Open My Savings Account

August 23, 2018

In my reading, my father told me that I need to have a plan and money to go to Arizona, not just wish it. He does not want me to fail. I need to start saving money for this *big move*. In my last reading, I was told I need at least six months of savings. Well, today was the day that I decided I was going to open up a saving account. I walked into Harford County credit union, signed in, and waited to be seen. A few minutes later, a loan officer called me into her office, and when I entered, I received a confirmation from my angels that I was moving in the right direction. Once in her office, I saw objects that reminded me of my future out west. I saw American Indian artifacts all over her office. There was a teepee, an American Indian woman photograph (her great-grandmother) bowls, a dreamcatcher, and a native blanket lying across her chair. I knew that I was at the right place and time. My dad is amazing. Angels are watching over me. Amen.

Angel in Prayer

August 26, 2018

Went to get some yogurt out of the refrigerator along with some granola to sprinkle on top and decided to eat it outside on the patio. I love the outdoors. As I am slowly taking my time and enjoying my yogurt, I noticed that there is an angel sitting on top of my yogurt in prayer. I had to look twice. I can clearly see her head bowed, hands together in prayer, and her small wings. A vision of beauty she is, and I feel so blessed to have seen this vision. Angels are amazing. Yes, I took a picture.

Image of Jesus

August 31, 2018

It was raining very hard and Geo and I were heading to Delaware Park Casino. Geo decided to listen to a new broadcast of Planet X. As we were listening, the announcer was painting a devastating picture of the world to come and how it was going to end for all of mankind. He was going into such very fine details of all the things that would occur before the end, and I was becoming very frightened about the future of this planet, and as the broadcast continued to play, a tractor trailer is now in front of us.

Come on, it's bad enough that it is raining really hard and visibility is low, and now we have a big square blocking our view. I tell Geo to go around it because I'm scared because I cannot see the road ahead, but he refuses. As we continued to drive, I noticed something on the back of the trailer that looks like a smudged cross. It is really raining hard, and it is hard to see it so I start videotaping it because I know that it is a cross, and I can get a better look on videotape because I can slow the image down. OMG! I looked at Geo, and I told him, "There is our answer! There is our answer! We will be fine! We will be fine!" We are receiving a sign from above that we will be okay. Jesus is telling me that we are going to be okay. Yes, I took pictures too. I love you, Jesus.

I look up, and I see number 44 on a license plate, I am receiving a sign from the angels confirming this. In the video, the truck is not sure if he will be able to pass under the bridge that is in front of him, for the bridge is low so he proceeds with caution and even sticks his head out the window to make sure; he even moves very, very slowly, even stopping as few times, but he makes it. Was that supposed to be another sign that we will make it through this darkness of Planet X? We followed this truck until it stopped raining, and then Geo decided to go around it. Was this another sign that through it all we will get through it? I believe yes, we will. God is amazing.

Make a Deposit

September 7, 2018

I went to the bank to make a deposit on my future it was only $9.34, but I made it a point to go, I was going to the library to return a DVD anyway, and it was one block away. As I was making my deposit, I looked up at the television screen behind the teller, and they're in capital letters it said ARIZONA! It was showing scores for whatever game was being played, but all I saw was *Arizona* in capital letters, and I knew it was a spiritual sign for me and a confirmation that I was going to Arizona. Thank you, angels.

God, Show Me a Sign You Love Me

September 12, 2018

Vanessa sends a picture and a text that a butterfly landed on Hollice's rosebush and flew away. It was beautiful, but I did not think anything of it because it was normal. Geo stayed home today, and we were hanging around the house all day, just relaxing when Geo walked to the sliding glass door and saw a butterfly and says, "God, show me a sign you love me by letting the butterfly land on my arm." He put out his arm, and the butterfly landed on it. He called me gently and said, "Maria, come quick," as I walked over the incident has already been over and he told me about it. I did not know if he was pulling my leg, so I questioned it in my heart and a moment later, I saw the butterfly on the gutter above my head. I put out my arm, and it went toward my arm and then flew away. I know that what Geo said really happened. I received confirmation from above. Angels are amazing.

A Portrait of Jesus

September 17, 2018

I was driving Cody home from driving lessons when I noticed someone in his complex was throwing away what seemed like everything they owed in the dumpster, and it was some really good stuff. My eldest daughter, Priscilla, is always looking for a great find so I decided to check it out for her. As I was looking over a dining set, a young man came out with more items to be thrown out. So I asked him what was going on and was he really throwing away all this good merchandise. He told me of the passing of his grandfather who he shared an apartment with while going to school here, but since he passed, he was moving back to Florida with his mom and stepdad, who was coming out of the apartment as we were talking.

The stepdad confirmed the story and invited me inside the apartment if I wanted to see more; he said everything must go, and everything was for free. I thought of my kids and agreed to see what more was waiting inside the apartment. I called my daughter immediately and took pictures of some of the items, which she was very much interested in and came up later to pick up. As I was looking around the apartment, my heart stopped; a portrait of Jesus captured my attention right away. It was the identical one that we had in my childhood home growing up.

As far back as I can remember, I always had a spiritual connection to this portrait of Jesus. I felt like he was speaking to me. When I became an adult, I told my mother that if she went before me that I wanted that portrait. Now twenty-plus years later, the universe is sending it my way. I was a little bit scared of being told no, but I quickly inquired about the portrait that was hanging on the wall. I even told them the story of how my mother has one, and I have never ever seen another one identical to it. The stepdad replied that they made so many of these back in the seventies, and they were really popular. He also told me that I could have it. I was so happy and grateful. I felt like I won the heaven lottery.

God is so amazing. I repeatedly thanked him and took the portrait off the wall. I wished them good luck in their travels back home and school. If it were not for me thinking of my daughter, I would have never stopped. Thank you, angels. This portrait will be with me forever, and I hope it will be passed on when I am gone. Angels are amazing. Amen.

Found a Dime

September 18, 2018

Geo and I pulled up to the Sunny Day Cafe to have breakfast; we parked and he got out to put coins in the meter and asked me if I had any coins, and I replied, "Not on me but in my money jar." But once I put them in that jar I cannot use them they go into my saving account. We entered the café, and I had to use the bathroom to wash up, and as soon as I entered the bathroom, there it was, a dime! I knew in an instant that it was my father confirming what I had told Geo about my coins. I was so happy and thanked him. Yes, I took a picture.

Message from Jesus

October 1, 2018

Got up this morning and went to pray by the portrait of Jesus; the sun was shining, and I always feel connected next to the image of him. As I was in prayer, I was also speaking to him about my life and where I wanted to be. I also asked him for a big and different kind of sign. I finished my prayers, got ready, and went to physical therapy. After signing in, I went to area where I always start my routine, and as I walked over, I noticed the word *God* on one of the other patient's shirt, and it got my full attention.

Now I wanted to know what it read because I asked Jesus in prayer for something *big* and different (but good) to happen to me today. After my first exercise was done, I was able to get close enough to read the back of the shirt fully; it read "Wherever God leads us," and the first thought I thought of was my prayer with Jesus just thirty minutes earlier. Now I couldn't wait for him to turn around just to see if he had something written on the front of the shirt. He turned around, and OMG! The front of his shirt read the following word *Arizona*! I knew at that instant moment I was receiving my answer to asking Jesus earlier for something big and different to happen to me. Jesus is amazing. Amen. Yes, I took a picture.

Rainbow for Angelo

October 13, 2018

My son Angelo just got a job driving cross America delivering fine art. I was so excited because he had told me he would be traveling out west and one of his stops would be Arizona! Angelo and I are texting every day. Every morning, I would ask Angelo what state are you in now? His reply today was "Your most favorite state." I was so excited and so happy that I could feel it in my whole body. He is in Tucson, Arizona, and it is sunny and beautiful. Later on in the day, it started to rain, and I was like it never rains in Arizona. I was a little disappointed because I really wanted my son to see why I love this state so much, and all of the sunshine it brings.

Well, later on in the day, at 5:42 p.m., I received a text from my son; he sent me a picture of a rainbow, and then a second picture with him and the rainbow while in the passenger seat of the truck. My reply was "Wow, wow" that is definitely, definitely a sign from my father to you. He then replied, "Yup, the biggest rainbow I have ever seen." I deeply believe in my heart that my father was communicating with my son through spirit world because this would be his future home. Pot of gold at the end of the rainbow. In two of my readings, my father specifically told me that Angelo would be one of my two children that would be moving to Arizona with me in the future.

Penelope at Hollywood

October 15, 2018

I had asked Penelope to spend the day with me today; it was my first day back to work since July 24, and I did not want to face it alone. That evening, Geo wanted to go to Hollywood Casino to play a little poker, so we went out. There was a beautiful sky setting, and I wanted to watch the colors of the nightfall, so I dropped him off at the front entrance of the building, and I told him I would be in later because I wanted to watch the skylight. I parked as far as I could away from the casino with its surroundings and as close to nature as I could get. As soon as I parked, I looked up, and I noticed a small tree that resembled an image of Penelope. The image was all in green and the surrounding grass was all yellow, which made her stand out. She was wearing her long dress and had angel wings. She was so beautiful I felt the urge to start praying, so I began to pray. I felt an overwhelming feeling that she was listening to me, and I could see twinkling lights where her eyes would be, I could also feel the presence of her in my heart. I'm so blessed to have her in my life. Thank you, Penelope. You are amazing. Yes, I took a picture.

Found a Feather

October 17, 2018

I was walking back to receiving, and a driver asked me about my absence, and then it turned to the subject of Arizona, and I told him I was leaving January 1, 2020, give or take, and while I was giving this date to him, I thought and felt a little doubtful because of my finances due to what happened to me in the months prior with surgery and the two months I did not get paid when I had my car accident, and as soon as I had this negative feeling inside me, I found a feather. It made me feel good inside, and I knew the angels were telling me everything would be okay. Angels are amazing. Yes, I took a picture.

Dream Big

October 18, 2018

It's that time again. I have to get a calendar for the receiving department, and I always get two, one for the office and one for me where I check in the vendors and small truck deliveries. I went out on the sales floor to get the calendars and club use them. I usually get a tropical calendar because it's filled with ocean pictures. Much to my amazement, this was the very first time ever that they did not have any tropical calendars delivered. So as I continued to look, I could not believe my eyes when I found the Grand Canyon on the cover of the 2019 calendar! On the front of it read "DREAM BIG" or medium, or whatever. It's your dream. I didn't think of it at first because I was too excited, but yes, it was a sign for me. Thank you, angels.

Slip and Fall

November 8, 2018

In my reading on Monday with Terry, my father told me I was to see a wet floor sign and that I was supposed to go around it at all cost, and if I did not, I would slip and chip my right elbow—ouch. My father was making a face and grabbing his elbow, and it was very painful. I know I have a habit of walking through a spill because I'm confident I won't fall, but now I'm scared, so I will walk around it as my father asked me too. I am forewarned!

When I was returning home from my reading, I had to stop by two stores, and both of them had a wet floor sign facing me as I opened the entrance door. There was no wet spill that I could see, though, I still stayed cleared of that area.

Well, today at work, I had to take a Safety Basic Training Quiz, and when I saw question no. 5, I was like, "No way." I am again being forewarned. Question no. 5: True or False? With any spill, you should block off the spill area to keep people from walking through it.

- True
- False

Yes, I took a picture, thank you, Terry; thank you, Dad.

Found a Dime

November 11, 2018

I was craving chocolate milk! I snuck out to go some, and when I arrived at the convenient shop, Geo had texted me and asked where I was at, and he added a list of items to get at the regular grocery store. I went in to grab my debit card, and it was not in my purse. I was panicking; where could it be? I was at the casino yesterday and left my purse next to Geo while he was playing poker. I looked at my M&T account online and no activity. It was very cold outside, and I gave up looking. I still had $2 cash in my car, so I decided to grab a small chocolate milk instead and look for it when I got home. Upon getting in my car, I looked at my father's picture that is in my car, and I asked him to help me find my card. I get home and got out of my car, and as I do, I noticed a dime in my seat. As my eyes continued to look further down, there under my seat, sticking halfway was my card! I knew that my father had helped me find it. Thank you, Dad, I love you. Yes, I took a picture.

It's Time...

November 24, 2018

We left the casino and it was after 1:00 a.m. and it was raining *very hard*, a total downpour, and visibility was low. We were driving home, and Geo was driving my car. As I was writing my entry about my spiritual encounter with Angel 12 this evening, a car caught my eye because it has been diving side by side with us for a few minutes now, and there were no other cars in the area; we were on Interstate 95. It's a four-lane highway.

The car was keeping up with us, sometimes a few feet in front of us and sometimes a few feet behind us, but always side by side with us in this heavy rain and it scared me. The car was yellow with white letters and multiple colors on the front and back, and it read something but with the heavy rain and the backsplash from the water on the road that is being thrown upward as we are driving made it hard to read.

I opened up the window to get a clearer look at what it says on the door panel, and as we got closer to it, I saw the writing on the side of the car. It reads, "It's TIME," and I knew in an instant that the angels again were telling me to start this book. Yes, I took a video of the car, and then it sped away. Angels are amazing.

Found a Dime

November 25, 2018

Went to Walgreens to return an item because I needed gas money to get to work and back. I walked up to the register to make my return, and as I was talking to the cashier, I looked down, and there it was, a dime! My father was here, and he knew what I was doing. I was surviving. I got myself out of the habit of worrying about money because every time I did, a dime would appear, and I knew it was a way of my father saying it is going to be okay. I love my father, and I am blessed to have him in my life, thank you, Dad.

Heart in the Sky

November 25, 2018

I received a call from my doctor's office, so I decided to take it outside, so I could be in private. I sat down on the bench and listened to the woman on the other end talking to me about my results of my test, and it is not good news for me. My thyroid was not working properly and my iron count is low, and they wanted me to take another blood drawing.

As I am listening to this, I am in tears about my health, and as I listened on, I look forward and straight ahead, and there in the sky right in front of me is a heart shaped cloud with an arrow through it, and my first instinct is "I am loved, and I will be okay." Yes, I took a picture. Thank you, angels.

Everything Will be All Right...

November 28, 2018

I have to transfer all my spiritual notes from my phone to a hard copy; the angels have been telling me that it is time. I have been getting signs from my last two readings and other signs, like the car that had written on its door panel "IT'S TIME." Cody and I were hanging out, and Cody wanted to go to Wegmans, which is in the same shopping center as Sprint, and I immediately knew this was a sign for me. I had to stop in there and ask them how to transfer notes from my phone to a hard copy.

Cody dropped me off in front of the Sprint store while he drove across the parking lot to Wegmans. It was such a magical evening as the blue in the sky was transitioning to a darker shade of blue, the twinkling stars were just slightly appearing and it was so still, and all I could here was the song "Three Little Birds" sung by Bob Marley. It was playing on one of the speakers outside of the shopping center.

In the lyrics, he said, "Every little thing will be all right," and I knew the angels were talking to me through his music. I know I will have this book done. My angels are guiding me. I have only ever heard this song one other time in my life when I was going through something else, and while at work, I heard this song come on. It was a sign for me then too. Yes, I videotaped the song playing while looking at the evening sky that evening. Angels are amazing.

Go with Big Red

January 4, 2019

It is 4:26 a.m. in the morning, and I am on Interstate 695 driving to work. A tractor trailer passed me on the right and on the back of the trailer it read, "Go with big red" I decided to take a picture of it because I knew it was a sign for me. Ten hours later at 2:49 p.m., Geo and I are at the Toyota center getting my oil change. As we entered the waiting area, they have snacks, red apples, and chocolate chip cookies, and I knew in that instant, I was to pick the red apple. My New Year's resolution this year was not to eat any sweets. Thank you, angels, for watching over me. Yes, I took a picture.

Found a Dime

January 15, 2019

Went to see a gastro-intestine doctor on December 5 because I have very low iron, and my primary doctor wants to rule out everything before they blame it on my heavy menstrual cycle. As I entered the examination room and sit down, I noticed two dimes on top of the sterile table where they keep their utensils on, and I asked the woman that is checking my vitals why are there two dimes on the sterile table, and she said that she does not know why. I knew why because I know that my father was with me and that everything will be okay.

As she finished up, I asked if I can take a picture of the dimes and she said yes. I then waited for the doctor to see me. On January 15, I have a follow-up appointment with the same gastro-intestine doctor as I entered the office I proceeded to go to the counter to sign in and there on the other side of the sliding glass window is a dime! It caught my attention immediately, and I knew that my father was once again with me and everything was going to be fine with me. Which it did end up being the case. Both my endoscopy and colonoscopy were normal. I love you, Dad, and thank you for caring about me. Yes, I took a picture of both the occurrence.

Found a Feather

January 22, 2019

It is so cold outside; it is literally freezing weather. I'm at work, and I had to go outside to bring in two carts of bakery stales that the volunteer could not take. It was so cold that I said to the angels out loud, "I don't want to work in this cold anymore. I don't want to be in this cold anymore. I want to work in the warm temperatures even if I have to work to the day I die. I just want to get out of here and have enough money to pack up and get a place to live."

As I finished saying this, out of nowhere, a tiny feather gently fell from the sky; no birds were in sight or around. I knew the angels were listening to my prayers.

Found a Dime

January 24, 2019

I was very, very hungry today and lucky to have $9.12 in my account, so I purchased a few slices of lunch meat and some bread from our club. As I stood in front of the register to purchase my two items, I found a dime; my father was watching over me. I love you, Dad.

Found a Dime

January 25, 2019

My son Cody bought his first car! It was a secret. I sort of found out about it from his older brother, Skyler. I went over to drop off a used laptop that I had gotten from a good friend of mine to help Cody with school work. When I got there, he showed me the car from the outside, and as I was looking inside of the driver's side window, I noticed a dime on the passenger side floor by the seat. I was so happy. The first I thought of was my father; he was here and he approved. Yes, I took a picture.

Found a Dime

February 6, 2019

I was on my lunch break talking with Vanessa and how proud of her I am because she is on a diet to lose thirty pounds before graduating on stage on May 24, and she has already lost seven pounds. As I was speaking with her, I found a dime, and I knew my father was listening to us, and he was very proud of her as well. Yes, I took a picture.

Found a Guitar Pick

February 17, 2019

Went to see my son Angelo today. He purchased a keychain for me from Arizona, and we started talking about his future, and he told me that he had a friend that offered him an opportunity to record in a studio. He had been writing songs and now has the chance to record them. I wished him luck, and I had to then leave because I had to get up early tomorrow for work.

I went to Giant food store to get a few supplies, and when I exited the store, it was still raining but a little harder now. As I took my first step off the curb, I noticed a small white object that was lying in the road with water running all over it. As I looked closer, I noticed it was a guitar pick! I knew it was a sign from the angels that Angelo was going to be successful in his music career. Thank you, angels. Yes, I took a picture.

American Indian

April 8, 2019

After depositing money into my Arizona account, I pulled out of the bank and drove up to the stop sign at the top of the small incline when I noticed an American Indian statue facing toward me. It was like he was confirming that I just deposited money in the bank. As soon as I got this thought in my mind, there coming in the opposite direction was a vehicle with the license plate no. 4444, and I know that Angel 4 was confirming my thought. I had never seen it there before, and I knew it was a sign from my angels that I am going to Arizona.

Arizona Tags

April 8, 2019

Yesterday, I texted a man that I met from Arizona, and I asked him how much is rent out there. He replied for a two-bedroom apartment it is around $2,000 a month. OMG, I was so discouraged and was brought down to hearing this. I still know that I am definitely, definitely going to Arizona. If I cannot afford Scottsdale, I just have to pick another city. I thought about this all day long, and I even asked a coworker who lived out there for fifteen years if this could be true. She said he was wrong and that she lived in Paradise City in a gated community, and it was way cheaper than that. It was still on my mind all day—Arizona, Arizona.

Well, as I'm coming home from work, I am only ten minutes away and this white car in front of me is going so slow. At first I get impatient but then think it's meant to me to go slow for a reason. Then I see it at the last second, it is totally out of place. It's a one in a million shot that I will ever see this again in my lifetime! There is a small, red, riding mower with an Arizona tag on it! I knew that sign was meant for me! It is a sign that I am going to Arizona, regardless! I made a U-turn, drove up the driveway, and I had to take a picture. I cannot make this stuff up. I might even call the person and see if they will sell me the license plate. Thank you, angels.

Found a Dime

April 9, 2019

I was on the dock sweeping, and it was so quiet you could hear a pin drop. I started to daydream of my future in Arizona, and as I was doing so, a dime showed up on the dock from nowhere. I knew that my father put it there for me to find. He knew what I was daydreaming about, and he was comforting and validating my daydream. Yes, I took a picture.

Be the Change

April 11, 2019

It wasn't until twenty-four hours later that I had noticed that I had received two signs not one on that day that I saw the Arizona license plate. I had called the number on the For Sale sign for the mower, and a man picked up. I told him that this was going to sound a little weird, but I believe in signs, and today I received another sign that I was going to move to Arizona because of the Arizona license plate on his mower, and I was not interested in buying the mower but was asking if I could buy the license plate. He replied, "You don't have buy it. I will give it to you."

I insisted, but he stayed firm. I asked if it was okay to pick it today, and he replied yes. I was so happy I was crying. Geo comes out of the shower, and I tell him what just happened in the last thirty minutes and that I going to get my very first Arizona license plate! He replied, "Let's go." I wanted to dress up because I wanted to take a picture with the nice man that was going to give me the tag. When we arrived, we met the two men; they were both retired, and one of them was visiting from Mesa Arizona! I told them I wanted to take a picture with them because they made me so happy, and because they had given me another sign I was going to Arizona! The man that was visiting had a shirt on that read, "BE THE CHANGE."

I have been saying for a long time that I want to change the world. I want to make it a better place. I want to get rid of hate in the world. I want to leave the world a better place. The angels are saying to me to "BE THE CHANGE."

Cody's Bible

April 17, 2019

Two days ago, my son Cody came over and surprised me; he looked very happy. Earlier in the day, I had asked him if he wanted to eat dinner with us, so I thought he was coming over to eat with us, but he was just stopping by. As I was putting the food on the plates, he asked me if I had a Bible, and I said yes, it was in one of my totes and he asked if he could have it. I told him yes. I would just have to find it. I also told him that the Bible was only $1 at the dollar store.

Cody called me today as I'm driving home from work and told me that he went to the dollar store the following evening to buy a Bible, but the dollar store had already closed so he decided to go to Walmart to buy it there; it was $19.99. He really did not have the funds to purchase it, so he had to transfer money from his savings account to his checking account to buy it. Today while he was at work, he found a $20 bill just lying on the floor of the building he was working in and he knew in an instant that he was being reimbursed from heaven. He took that $20 and put it toward a tank of gas, which was much needed. Thank you, angels. Thank you for looking after my son, Cody.

Optical Repair Shop

May 13, 2019

We have an optical center inside our club, and every single day for the last year, they send out a package to a repair shop that it is located in of all places Phoenix, Arizona. I get so excited just knowing that it is going to Arizona, and almost every day we receive a package from them that has been repaired and shipped back. I get even more excited when it gets returned, knowing that it has actually been in Arizona. One day, I even wrote a tiny message on the outside of the box hoping to get a reply back that read, "I am coming out there" (with a smiley face on it). I know that this is a definitely another a sign from the angels for me that I am moving out west.

Angels are amazing.

Cross through the Trees

May 16, 2019

Another beautiful sun setting, and I asked Geo if we could go watch it. We went to our usual place, but lately we have been parking in a different spot. As we are watching the sun setting, we can hear the birds softly singing; it was so peaceful. I took out my phone and started videotaping. As I'm videotaping, I noticed there is a cross within the trees. It is clear as day, and I pointed it out to Geo who also saw it right away, and I knew it is a sign from above. Thank you, Jesus. Amen.

Believe

May 18, 2019

I have not been working Saturdays for a very long time but was asked to today because the regular person was on vacation. I walked into the building and proceeded to go to the front of the building to punch in when I noticed a blue sticker on the floor. After I punched in, I decided to go back to see what the sticker says because I know it was a sign for me. The sticker read "BELIEVE," and the first thing came to my mind was *I'm going to the Karma Fest today, and I should believe what I will see.*

Hours later, Geo and I are at the festival, and there were crystals and mediums and all sorts of interesting things to see. There was also a free spiritual reading. I decided to have a reading. An older woman and a young man sat around me; they were just spiritual guides, not mediums or psychics. They just gave me some insight on general information. At the very end, the young man asked if he could say a prayer for me, and I said yes. This prayer was so powerful that I could feel the energy on me, and I felt like a band was lifted off me; it was incredible he was asking the Holy Spirit to help me in my journey in life and to unblock me. After he had said this prayer, I remembered the word "BELIEVE" that I saw this morning. The angels were telling me to believe what this man had said to me in prayer. Yes, I took a picture with him.

I Like to Change the World

May 21, 2019

I was on the road and heading to work. I was in prayer; I wanted to change the world and make it better than how I came into it. I have been saying this for a while now, and then something told me to turn the radio on, and I heard the last line of this song, "I'd love to change the world but I don't know what to do so I leave it up to you." It was like the radio was speaking to me through spirit. It totally reminded me of myself because I want to change the world, and I don't know how and in prayer, I usually ask Jesus to give me a sign or use me as a vessel to help do the Lord's work. The actual song is titled "I'd Love to Change the World" by Ten Years After; it was the first time I'd ever heard this song—beautiful song. Angels are amazing.

Vanessa's Graduation

May 24, 2019

What a totally *beautiful day* today was! I woke up to a beautiful sunny day with a perfect breeze and a bright blue sky. I told Geo what a perfect day for Vanessa's graduation. I checked my balance, and it was $544. I said my prayers, and I told my father I wanted him to be with us all day, and then I kissed his picture.

We went to breakfast, returned, got dressed, and we went to get flowers. As we drove, I saw Angel 44 on three license plates. We got the flowers, tissues, and a few snacks for Geo, went to the register to pay. The woman in front of us wanted her discount, so she pushed the help button. Woman came over, fixed the issue, and when she did, I looked at her total. It was $4.44. I was so excited; the angels were here with me. Then it was my turn. I purchased my flowers and snacks total ending in 44 cents.

As we walked out, something told me to ask Geo, "Are the tissues in the bag?" They were not. I needed tissues because I knew I was going to cry at the ceremony. We went back in, and I noticed that Geo had moved the box away from the belt and placed them on a self-standing sunglass rack, which was why I forgot the tissues. I was a little upset because we were on a timed schedule. I forgot at that moment that everything is for a reason because if I hadn't gone back in the store, I would not have noticed a tattoo raven the length of this man's lower leg who was checking out at the register.

I was so excited because I knew my father was with me! I explained to the man that my father sent me ravens from heaven and asked if I could take a picture of his tattoo and he was happy too. OMG, I was so excited. Then as we proceeded to the exit door, and there it was—a dime. My father is here; my father is here. He will be with us. I was so grateful. We picked up my mother, and as we drove, I saw Angel 44 over four more times. Angels are among us. We arrived at the university; we are now looking for seats. Finally we find seats; Hollice (Vanessa's boyfriend) led the pack. He sat followed by Geo, and then it is supposed to be my mother but she decides to sit on the end seat because she is tired and needs more room so I am to take that seat. I sat down and start to feel below my seat to see if there is space so I can put my purse there when I feel a metal piece and decide to look to see what it is. It's a shiny piece of gold metal attached to the seat that gives the seat number and mine reads four.

Angels are here with me. After the ceremony, the graduates exit first, then the families. Vanessa called me and said there are four sections and she was in section 4. Angels are with us. We head to dinner—best dinner ever! After dinner, we get into the car, and as we were driving, I see a raven in the sky, wings spread. I even see a sign that reads "Phoenix" (I see the word *Phoenix* everywhere, are the angels telling me I am moving to Phoenix, Arizona?). Then to top the evening, after we dropped off my mother, and we are pulling into Delray Court, there in the sky, I see an angel with large wings and its knees bent. What a vision of love, what a perfect day. I really enjoyed all of you being with me on this very special day today and *always*. Yes, I took pictures. I am truly blessed. Thank you, angels. Thank you, Dad, I love you.

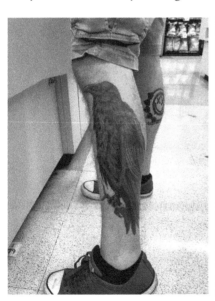

Angel Rock

June 2, 2019

Geo wanted to go to Hollywood casino to play some poker, so I dropped him off and go run some errands. It is calling for rain later, so I decided to stay outside a little longer by sitting in my car and enjoying the beautiful weather while it lasted. It was so peaceful, and there were so many beautiful white rocks lining the parking lot where it met the grass. I decided to see if any of them capture my attention. I started picking up rocks that I like and have been setting them aside. It has been an hour now, and a certain white rock captured my attention; it was not laying where all the other rocks were. As I am walking toward it, I started seeing an image of an angel on it. OMG, there was an image of an angel on it. I took a picture and felt a connection to it, so I took it home with me. Angels are amazing.

I'm Blessed

June 4, 2019

We went to have dinner with Geo's younger daughter and her boyfriend; when we pulled up to the parking lot, I noticed a tire cover on a Jeep that read "I'm blessed." It was so pretty I wanted to take a picture of it, but it was awkward because we all met outside, so I did not. I thought about it all through dinner that I should have taken a picture of it and was hoping that it would still be there once we left. After dinner, Geo wanted to go to the movies and asked his daughter if they would like to join us; they declined, so we exited the building alone and no Jeep was to be found. We arrived at the movie theater, and as we were getting out of the car, I noticed it! The car right next to us had a sticker on the window of their car that also read "I'm blessed," and I knew that message was for me and that the universe was sending it to me again. Angels are amazing. Yes, I took a picture.

Found a Dime

June 13, 2019

I was on my lunch break and walking through the Toyota parking lot when I found a dime. I knew my dad was with me and that he knew that I had to take my mother to the MVA right after work so she could renew her identification ID.

Found a Dime

June 14, 2019

Cody and I were going out to lunch, and I was thinking and worrying about money again, and then I found a dime, and I knew my father was telling not to worry. Yes, I took a picture.

Arizona Angel

June 15, 2019

We are at Delaware Park Casino, and Geo is playing poker while I am sitting behind him and talking to a young man to his right about poker in Vegas, which then turned into talking about Arizona. He told me he has a best friend who moved out there to be closer to his children; he also added that his friend is super nice and lonely and would love to have us as guests in his home. He then gave me his number and told me to give him a call. I was so excited when I saw his number; it has 444 in it   that's my angel number (angel no. 4). Angels are amazing. We just finished playing poker with a win, and we are now driving home, and I decided to text him; his name is Frank. We are texting back and forth just a brief introduction and light conversation before we ended the chat. As soon as we finished texting, a car jumped in front of us with Arizona tags!

I cannot make this stuff up. Yes, I took a picture, and I just had to send it to him too; he replied, "That's so crazy." I knew that was a sign for me.

Blessed Mother Mary Visits Me

June 18, 2019

As we were driving home from the reservoir, we had to pass the statue of the Blessed Mother that I always pass by to and from work each day. I decided to drive on the lot to show Vanessa the statue. After we pulled up, I decided to get out of my car and say a prayer to her. I walked up to her, and I kneeled. As I started to say a little prayer, I was noticing how beautiful the orange flowers were around her feet. They were so rich in color and so bright that I could not take my eyes off them. I did not take a picture because we were on a tight schedule. Vanessa had a doctor's appointment and my phone was in the car.

I decided to get in the car and head home. As we walked into the house, there in front of my very own eyes, I saw the same exact color flowers that were by the Blessed Mother Mary's feet. Geo had surprised me with flowers. My very first instinct was the Blessed Mother Mary had come home with us! It was such a warm, peaceful, and joyous feeling inside my soul. I am so blessed. I was so excited that I pointed out the flowers to Vanessa who also saw the flowers at the statue. Yes, I took multiple pictures, and then the next day after work, I stopped by the statue to take pictures of the same color flowers there. Blessed Mother Mary is amazing.

Angel in the Tree

June 22, 2019

Geo and I were heading out to a party, and we were taking a scenic way. As we were driving, something told me to look out the side window, and when I did, I noticed an angel! It was in the group of trees but way darker, so it really caught my attention. I quickly asked Geo to turn the car around, so I could get a picture. Angels are amazing.

My Three Signs

June 25, 2019

I was briefly doubting my Arizona dream because of lack of money. I felt like I might have to push it back a little. At my reading, on Tuesday by Terry, best physic/medium ever, I was told I was going to meet three people that were from Arizona or three things Arizona before the end of this week. This was going to be validation that everything was going as scheduled. The following day, June 26, while at work, one of my managers called me over; she was in a conversation with another employee, and they were talking about the weather out west, and they wanted my input. My coworker then added that her son was in Arizona as we speak. I said, "Arizona? Why didn't you tell me?"

My imaginary tail was wagging! I was so excited! I asked her how does he like it, and she replied, "He loves it." She also added that he sent her a boomerang video of the Grand Canyon. Ooooh, I wanted to see it. I then asked for her to send it to me. I quickly thought about the prediction that Terry (best psychic/medium ever) said, but at the time, I still thought it was going to be three people. *(I was wrong this was my first Arizona sign that I was going!)* End of the day, and I am pulling into the driveway, I decide to stop while still in the car and pull out mail from the mailbox. I put the mail on my lap and briefly look at it all, I see is bills, bills, bills, and then I come across a personal letter addressed to me from Peter (a beautiful and special friend of mine)! I got so excited and finish pulling into the driveway, go inside and quickly open my letter; oh my god, it is an article about *Arizona*! It's a sign; it's a sign! I was so excited! I had to call him and tell him about my reading.

He said that the article was in the papers and he wanted to send it to me. I love you, Peter. Later that day, my son Cody had a doctor's appointment and him being a minor, I have to be there. I had to get iced coffee because we were out, and I decided to go to ShopRite instead of our regular grocery store because it was right next door to the doctor's office. As I am walking around the store, I see a huge display of Arizona Tea, it was like four pallets long! It repeated the words *Arizona, Arizona, Arizona* over and over and over again. My heart was beating hard and fast with excitement. This was a huge validation sign that I was going to Arizona and the third sign Terry my physic/medium and friend had told me in my reading. Angels are amazing. Terry is amazing.

Are You Ready?

June 26, 2019

While I'm driving home from work, a truck goes by me with a question written on its side that reads "Are you redi?" The first thing that came to my mind is my future out west, and I said, "Yes, I am ready" out loud. Yes, I took a picture. Angels are amazing.

Raven Image in the Sky

July 2, 2019

I had just dropped off Skyler at his friend's house (he was getting his drive time in), and as I was getting into the driver's seat I see an image of the raven in the blue sky, surrounded by the white clouds. I could clearly see the image, beak, and wings spread wide open. I told my son that my dad was watching over us. Yes, I took a picture.

Found a Dime

July 2, 2019

I am at Giant and worried about money, which I have not done in a while I am going through half and half, like its water and it is very expensive. I'm not saving any money for my future, and as soon as I thought this, I found a dime. My dad is here with me.

Television Box Arizona

July 5, 2019

A fifty-inch TV came in UPS; it is addressed to the GM. I called and asked him about it, and he replied, "It is the TV that was ordered for the break room." He also added, "Hold it in the cage until next Friday when they come in to install it." I noticed an Arizona image on the box right away and it made me happy.

A month later, I noticed the word *Westworld* on the right-hand corner written in small letters. I'm going to live in the west world. The box is a sign from the angels, the box has now been with me over two months, and it is a daily reminder to me of where I am going to be in the future. Thank you, angels; you are keeping my vision of Arizona alive. Yes, I took a picture.

Angel and the Dime

July 5, 2019

Andy and I are sitting on the bench outside next to the pavilion tent and talking about his repeated dream of him dying, and I assure him a dream of dying as a sign of long life. As he is telling me the dream, I can see an angel in the cloud behind him. I tell him that a loved one is listening to him and watching over him. I also tell him that he would receive a sign from a loved one by the end of this evening or first thing in the morning hour.

After we spoke for a minute (LOL, almost two hours), I have to run because it's after 9:00 p.m., and Geo is probably wondering where I am, and Andy has to work the next day. He decided to walk me in, and as we are walking, I see a dime! "Quick squat." I tell him and pointed to a dime, "I want to take a picture with you and the dime." My father is here. Now that I look back at this moment, I wonder if the dime was supposed to be for him. It was on his side of the walkway. I just saw it first, so I thought it was for me. I will call him tomorrow. I believe in my heart it was supposed to be for him.

Guitar Water Stain

July 8, 2019

I was walking to the back of the club when I see a water stain that resembles a guitar and the first thing I think of is my son Angelo! OMG! I have to call Angelo and check in on him. Later in the day, I texted him if he wanted to come over and have dinner with us. He said yes and had dinner with us for two nights in a row. I knew this was a sign for me from the angels to see my son. Yes, I took a picture.

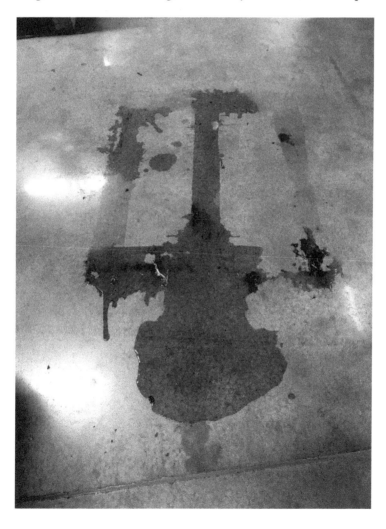

Doorbell Rings, Who Is It?

July 13, 2019

It was early Saturday morning, and I was covering a shift for one of my coworkers who was on vacation. The last vendor just finished packing out his product and returned to the receiving dock. He was so excited to get the day over with because he was going to be playing at the Caribbean festival in Baltimore.

As we continued to talk, the conversation turned spiritual. We both believe and have a connection to the spirit world, and I feel very comfortable talking to him. I started talking about my father when the receiving doorbell rang. I took one step forward and pulled back the thermal, plastic, frosted, colored curtains, which kept the cold in the building and looked out, but there was no one there. I stepped back in and looked through the large window that was built into the door to see if whoever rang the bell might have quickly jumped in the building and was waiting for me to buzz them in, but again, there was no one there.

I then opened the one-way door and looked into the receiving office to see if anyone walked in there really quick, but again, no one was there either. Another thing that was unexplainable was that even if someone rang the bell and ran off we would have seen them 100 percent because there is nowhere to hide; it is an open area. Now both the vendor, and I heard it and this doorbell can also be heard all the way to the front of the building. This was unexplainable to the both of us. I then knew it had to be my father. I was talking about him at the time this happened, and my vendor also believes that it was him visiting me. My dad is amazing; angels are amazing. Amen.

Found a Dime

July 17, 2019

I have a doctor's appointment today. It's for my swollen legs. I swear it's my thyroid medication I was on because I have never had this problem before, but for peace of mind, and I have health insurance, I will get it checked out. Well, this morning at 9:52 a.m., I see a dime, and I know that I will be fine. My father is with me. Then at 12:13 p.m., as I'm leaving early to go to this appointment, I see another dime. My father was going with me. Yes, I took a picture. Thirty minutes into the ride, I saw the number 44 on a tracker trailer, and I knew that the angels are also with me. Eleven minutes later, I was at the doctor's office, and as I was looking for a parking spot, there was Angel 44 and I was parking right next to it unintentionally, and I definitely know that the angels were going in with me to get it checked out. Thank you, spirit world, for loving me.

Found a Penny and a Dime

July 23, 2019

Tomorrow is my father's birthday, the big eighty-two! Wow, he is getting old! This morning, Geo texted me that there were twelve ravens on the lawn chair. It was odd; he also said there was no food and the cat was not even out. I believe it was a sign. He then said maybe because it was my father's birthday; I told him that my father's birthday was tomorrow.

Well, later on, I was walking into my area of work, and behind the door, a very shiny penny caught my eye, and I thought of Penelope. Now as I was walking up front to punch out for lunch, I found a dime. I know that I am to see my father today. I was looking forward to going tomorrow on his actual birthday, but I have a doctor's appointment tomorrow for a procedure I am having done, and I have to be cleared for surgery so I will have to go today. I love you, Dad. I believe he sent me the ravens today because he knew I couldn't go tomorrow, and he was acknowledging it.

A Dime and a Cactus Balloon

July 23, 2019

Today, I received two signs: a dime from my father, and when I went
to Giant, I saw a cactus balloon. Is that an Arizona sign or what? I
asked the lady in the flower shop, how often do you get cactus bal-
loons? She said it was the very first time that they ever came in and
that she got six of them and they all sold out but that one. I knew
that was supposed to be for me to see, it put a smile on my face and
heart. Yes, I took a picture.

Happy Birthday, Dad

July 24, 2019

Today is my father's birthday! I know that I will receive a sign from him today. At 7:27 a.m., I found a dime, and then at 1:38 p.m. while driving home, I saw an angel on his knees in the clouds praying, then another angel at 2:53 p.m. in the clouds praying. I then entered the craft store at 3:11 p.m. and a sign caught my attention; it read, "Family is the greatest blessing." I was definitely receiving a message from my father today on his birthday. Yes, I took a picture. Later on that evening, I received a breathtaking sunset, which I shared with our family cat, Roscoe. Thank you, Dad. I love you.

Angel 44 and the UPS Man

July 25, 2019

The last few times we have had a UPS truck with the number 44 in the license plate but always a different driver in it. Well, today it was magical the UPS truck pulled up, and on the side of the truck it had the number 44 on it. The number was actually 447, another angel number of mine. As I went to take a picture of the truck, the driver came out and saw me. I quickly explained to him that 44 is my angel number.

As I told him this he said that he sees that number *everywhere*!

"No way," I said. "I see that number everywhere too." He then went on and told me of everywhere he sees it. I told him what Angel 44 means. I told him I was writing a book and if I could take a picture of him and put it in my book, and he said yes. Every Thursday, we receive our books in and if the order is under $500 UPS brings it in. The boxes always have red stripes on them, but the number of boxes changes every week. They are labeled as follows, for example, if they are three boxes, then they are labeled 1 of 3, 2 of 3, 3 of 3. The number of boxes for today's delivery was forty-four boxes. I cannot make this stuff up! I told the driver, "You even brought me boxes with the number 44 on them." Angels are amazing.

Spiritual Gift on Procedure Day

August 2, 2019

Having a procedure to stop heavy menstrual flow. As I entered the hospital, I am greeted by a very nice older woman behind the counter. She took my name and Geo's name and gives me instructions and then hands me a spiritual gift; it is a finger rosary ring, and I know that everything will turn out well with my procedure. Earth angels are everywhere. Next thing I know, I wake up in recovery room no. 4; angels are amazing. The procedure was a success. Thank you, Jesus. Thank you, angels. Yes, I took a picture.

Angel 444

August 9, 2019

We are heading to get a snowball before we head out to Delaware Park. As we are cutting through the neighborhood, that's when I see it, a license plate that reads Angel 444; this is definitely an angel sign for me. I asked Geo to please turn around so I could take a picture of it.

Amen, Lord, amen, thank you. We then proceed and then arrive at Delaware Park. I drop off Geo at the entrance, and I went to park. As I'm looking for a parking spot, I see Angel 444 once again. Angels are amazing; yes, I took a picture.

Arizona Tags

August 23, 2019

This morning on my way into work, I had to get this song out of my head before I could start to pray. I turned on the radio for a few minutes to change my mindset. As I continued to drive, I thought about all the messages of positivity and keep going forward all at the same time I'm thinking about when I'm leaving my employer and how much money I have saved up so far. I still need to pay off my car and also think about car insurance, gasoline, and future maintenance for my car. I am feeling a little discouraged. Can I pull this off? Money is always short. I clear my head and start to pray. I am now on the last stretch of the road, which dead ends at a large cul-de-sac right before entering the parking lot. There I see a tractor trailer with Arizona tags. I have been driving this road for twenty-six years and have never seen a tractor trailer with Arizona tags. I definitely know this was a sign from the angels telling me that I am going to Arizona. Thank you, angels, I needed that. Yes, I took a picture.

Raven Appears around Cooler

Came into work this morning and quickly found out that all the boxed coolers for the meat department were down because of a storm we had overnight, which cut out all the power to them. Now all the food in those coolers had to be immediately loaded into grocery carts, shrink-wrapped in plastic and put into the big, room size, cooler that was not affected by the storm outage. I volunteered to help out; it was going to be a lengthy project, and we only had four hours until the store opened. As I was loading up the carts with product, I knew there was a few drops of water from the cases defrosting, but I did not pay attention to it because it was only a couple drops. It's like when you wash your hands and you walk over to grab a hand towel and a couple drops of water land on the floor.

Well, to my surprise, when I was done emptying out the case and stepped away, I saw a raven looking back at me! I could see its eye, beak, feet, and wings clearly and this was a water stain below me. I was so super happy that my father had visited me that I quickly called over the meat manager to show him. I told him that my father had visited and sent me a raven. My father is amazing! Yes, I took a picture.

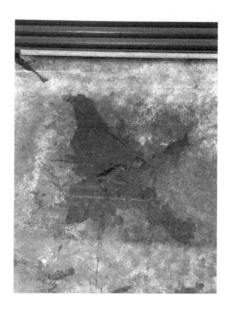

Pot of Gold

August 23, 2019

As the day progressed at work, I found a gold plastic coin with a picture of a trunk full of coins on it. I, again, knew it was another sign from the angels that I would be financially okay. Thank you, angels. Yes, I took a picture.

"We Will Bring You There"

August 25, 2019

Cody left very late to head down to Ocean City for a few days, and I was worried because most of his driving would be in the dark, and he was fairly a new driver. I told him to promise me that he would call me when he arrived. I had to go to sleep because I had to get up at 3:45 a.m. for work. That night, I had a dream of a pumpkin and a voice that spoke to me and said, "We will bring you there." The next thing I knew was waking up to the sound of the alarm going off and Cody never calling.

I picked up my phone to see if he had left me a message, it read, "I made it." I was so relieved. I then understood my dream. The orange pumpkin represents my son Cody, for he has orange hair or as we call it rust color or ginger, as his brother calls him sometimes. The phrase "We will bring you there" was the angels telling me that they were guiding Cody as he drove by himself to the ocean for the very first time alone. Angels are a blessing to my life. Thank you, angels, for watching over my son.

Raven at the Beach

September 7, 2019

Weekend getaway to Atlantic City, New Jersey, and nothing like a sunrise on the beach.

Geo is leading the way. I like to sometimes walk slower to see if any seashell catches my eye. As we continued to walk, I see a very shiny penny on the sand, and I quickly think of Penelope, my spirit guide. I think it is sort of odd finding a penny on the beach because I have never seen this. We continued walking; Geo was still leading the way. A few minutes later, I see a dime! I quickly call over Geo to tell him that there is a dime on the beach; my dad is here. Can this be? I have never seen a dime on the beach.

So I then question it and asked Geo if he had put the dime there, and if he did, it was not funny. In his normal nonexcited voice, he said he did not put it there. I still did not believe him and asked him to empty out his pockets. Both his pockets were empty. So out loud, in my native Sicilian tongue, I asked my father if he had put the dime there or not because I did not believe Geo, and if he sent it to me, then I wanted to see a sign. As God as my witness, two minutes later, there on the beach lands a raven! A *raven*! It landed right in front of me. I cannot make this stuff up. I am so lost for words at this moment in time. Geo was in disbelief also. My dad is confirming to me that it is he that sent me that dime. My father is so amazing; he even sent a heart for me. I love you, Dad. I took a picture and video-taped this moment that will forever live in my heart.

Free Parking Ticket

September 9, 2019

Had an appointment with my lawyer today to go over some stuff, and I hate to pay a parking fee when I'm living paycheck to paycheck; it's such a waste of money. I thought about it all day, and I don't know why, but I did. After work, I drove to the lawyer's office, and as I was looking for a spot to park, an elderly couple pulled up next to me and asked if I wanted their parking ticket, which still had a lot of time on it. I quickly accepted and thanked them for their kindness; they handed me the ticket, and they drove off. God bless them. I looked at the ticket. It had $10 remaining on it, so I have plenty of time at the lawyer's office. Thank you, angels, for listening to my prayer. Yes, I took a picture, angels are amazing.

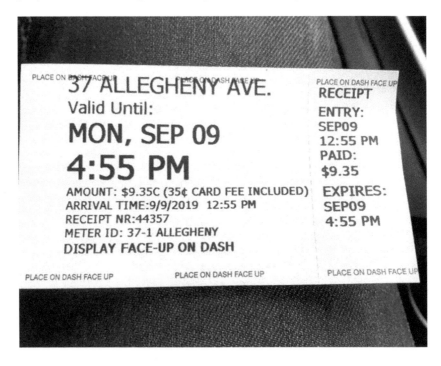

Angel 44

September 10, 2019

I was taking a shopping cart with old worn-out tires out to the tire trailer to be disposed of. I have something on my mind, but I cannot remember what it is. As I approached the trailer, I noticed that Angel 44 is here. Angels are amazing and always around us, thank you. Yes, I took a picture.

Found a Pendant with Cross

September 16, 2019

Very early this morning, as I was walking across the parking lot heading into work, I stepped on something small but hard that got my attention. I could not really see clearly what it was because it was still dark outside, but it was a religious pendant. As I came into the light of the building, I could see it much clearer. It was a special pendant with a simple cross on one side and the blessed Mother Teresa on the other side. What a blessing to find. Mother Teresa was an Albanian-Indian, a Roman Catholic nun, a missionary, and now a saint. What a blessing from above. Angels are amazing. Yes, I took a picture. Amen.

Happy Birthday, Angelo

September 21, 2019

Today is Angelo's birthday; my eldest son turned twenty-three! We are at the casino, and I find a dime, and I know it's my father wishing him a happy birthday; he always also sends me dimes on all my kids' birthdays and other special occasions. Yes, took a picture. My dad is amazing. I love you.

Found a Feather

September 24, 2019

As we were leaving my aunt's home, I saw a feather, and my daughter said she saw one every time we go see her. I know my aunt is an earth angel, and I can still remember as a child, it is she that taught me how to make the sign of the cross and taught me how to pray. In Italian, of course. Amen.

Trying to Save Roscoe

September 26, 2019

I called the vet today because our family cat, Roscoe, is not well. A woman picked up; her name is Angel. Is that a sign? As I was speaking with her about his condition, a dragonfly flew in through the open bay door and started buzzing loudly. Is this also a sign? While I am trying to figure this situation out, I also saw a white feather. A white feather symbolized light and love.

Angels Answer, "Anyway You Want It"

September 30, 2019

Driving home from Target, I have the radio on, which I seldom do and the song "Wrapped around Your Finger" by The Police is playing. As it is playing, I am thanking the angels and spirit world for letting me see the Arizona tag in the parking lot. As I'm praising them, the song ended and the next thing I heard was "Anyway You Want It" by Journey. The angels were responding to me. Angels are amazing.

Stink Bug Silences Me

October 2, 2019

I am kneeling at the bedroom window talking to Cody who was outside parked on the street working on his car, which keeps overheating. I feel sorry for my son because I cannot financially help him fix the car, and I know he needs a car for work. I, as his mother, then told him I have my Arizona fund money that I cannot really touch, but I will loan him the money but I need to be paid by the end of next week. As I am saying this, as God as my witness, I could see a stink bug literally flying in slow motion toward my face. It landed right on the screen where my mouth was at; if it was not for the screen, it would have landed in my mouth. Oh my god. I said to Cody, "Did you see that?" He nodded yes. At first I don't think about it, and then the thoughts come into my head my father is quieting me; he is stopping me from speaking. My father does not want me to touch this money at all. I tell Cody this. I tell him, "See how the spirit world works!" I want to take a picture, but I am in a state of mind of stillness at this moment then the stink bug flies off and lands on the rooftop. They usually stay in one place for hours. After the moment is finished, I go get my phone and take a picture. My dad is amazing, and he really wants me to succeed. I love you, Dad, thank you.

I'm Home

October 4, 2019

Driving to Atlantic City while watching a rock video that my brother just sent me that was videotaped in Arizona. I told Geo, "I want a house out here," showing him a desert scene from the video with nothing around but sand for miles and miles. He replied, "How will you get your groceries?" I told him, I will worry about that later, LOL. I told him I am looking forward to being a spirit one day so I can always be out there. As soon as I said this, a car goes by with a license plate that reads "IM HOME" OMG! I cannot make this stuff up! Angels are listening. Yes, I took a picture.

Are You an Angel?

October 7, 2019

I am on the phone with my younger daughter Vanessa, and I am venting about my mother. As I was complaining a car in the opposite direction caught my eye; the license plate reads "R U ANGEL" and I knew right away that the angels were talking to me in spirit, and they were disappointed in me. I also felt a feeling of "I should be a better human." It all happened in a blink of an eye. I quickly told my daughter what just happened. I then quickly changed my demeanor. Thank you, angels.

Found Two Dimes to Cheer Me Up

October 8, 2019

Not too happy today. First I had a driver on my rear as I was pray-ing. Then I went to have my reading with Terry, and she showed me a picture of a license plate that she had seen earlier today that read "WAHOO 21." She told me that was the year I was moving to Arizona. I was very disappointed in hearing this, and I asked her if that was what my father had told her. She said that my father told her that I did not save enough money to go. I then was thinking I do not want to leave in 2021. I want to leave in 2020.

I don't wanna be here another year. I cannot stand it here. I am not in a good mood thinking about it. Also it sucks not having enough funds to have my dream come true sooner. After my reading was over, I headed home, and on the way, I had to make one stop at Wawa, and that's when I saw it, a dime, it made me know that my father is here, but I'm not feeling it (happiness). A few minutes later, I find another dime. I know my father is trying to cheer me up. It did make me smile because he tried twice, and I know he is with me; I just cannot hear or see him. I love you, Dad, and I know you are only looking out for your daughter. Thank you for loving me. Yes, I took a picture.

Signs of Az, I'm Going

October 8, 2019

Around 11:30 a.m., a truck pulled up in receiving to pick up an order, and I will be the loader. I noticed right away that the truck has an Arizona license plate. It's a sign for me; I know it is. Two hours later, while driving home, I see a magnet on the side of a car that reads "AZ battery rescue." I know that's another sign for me that I am going to Arizona. I then see a lady bug (make a wish). You know what I wished for, this is spiritual sign I am going to Arizona. I then arrive at the grocery store to pick up a few things, and I am in the paper goods isle, and I see a tissue pack which says, "Believe in yourself." Thank you, angels. I needed that. *Amen.*

Yes, I took pictures.

Found a Black Feather

October 9, 2019

I AM SO UPSET. I received a letter from my lawyer today; it was disturbing. I was in rage. They have set a pretrial conference date of May 29, 2020, and a trial date of July 7–8, 2020. I am leaving Maryland in January, and I never wanna come back! I am so upset! I am not going to stand for it! Evil needs to be destroyed! Richard admitted fault; he was a man, and I respect him for that. It's the insurance company that is playing their tricks. God help me; I am so angry. We are driving to Delaware Park so Geo can place a sports bet. I stayed in the car. Now we are riding back, and we are only fifteen minutes away from the house, but I really need to use the bathroom. I drank too much iced coffee. We pulled into the Royal Farms, and I quickly ran in the use the bathroom, and then as I exit the building and started walking to the car, I stepped off the curb at the exact place that there is a very large black feather; it is almost twelve inches long lying in the street. I know that the angels sent me this feather, and I also know that a black feather is a sign of protection. Thank you, angels. I picked it up, and I know that I am protected. Yes, I took a picture.

Later on that evening, I received a text message from a special friend, Peter. It read, "THOSE WHO LEAVE EVERYTHING IN GOD'S HAND WILL EVENTUALLY SEE GOD'S HANDS IN EVERYTHING." He did not know what had happened to me that day.

Angels are amazing spiritual beings. Peter is an amazing human, thank you.

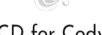

CD for Cody

October 12, 2019

Geo and I were having lunch when I received a call from Cody; he had just had a fender bender with my car, and he was very upset. I exited the restaurant because I cannot hear with the live music playing inside and asked him if he and the car are okay. They were both fine. I tried to calm my son down, but he is so upset; it's making me upset. As we are in conversing back and forth, the song in the background playing is "Everyone knows that it will be all right." Oh my God, I cannot make this stuff up. I start to tear up. Next thing I know is the young man who is singing and playing this song on his guitar turned around and asked me if everything is okay. (I did not know that the window had no glass in it.) I really started to tear up now, and I told him what had just happened. He asked me if he could give me a CD to give to my son, and I said yes. I knew it was a sign from the angels. Angels are amazing; this young man is amazing, and he was also an earth angel. Yes, I took a picture and video. Thank you, angels. We then left the restaurant, and twenty minutes into the ride, I saw black feathers taped to a telephone pole, and I knew my son was protected. Black feather meaning, a sign of protection.

Signs of Love

October 12, 2019

Later that evening, Geo took me to see a sunset because I was upset with what happened with my son earlier in the day, and he did not want to see me down. As we were watching the sun as it was setting, we saw a heart-shaped rock and a rainbow on a sunny evening, and I knew these were signs from the angels. I am loved; thank you, angels. Yes, I took a picture.

Raven in My Car

October 16, 2019

I'm at Giant picking up some items, and as I returned to my car, it was wet outside. I get into my car and see what resembles a raven silhouette on the floor mat of my car. Oh my god, it is! I cannot make this stuff up! It's my father visiting me. God is amazing. My dad is amazing. Yes, I took a picture.

Red Lizard

October 17, 2019

On my lunch break, and as I am walking, I see it: a red lizard, and the first thing I think of is "I AM GOING TO ARIZONA." It's a sign! I am so happy! The last time I saw this same-looking red lizard was the day before I went to Arizona for the very first time (2016). God is amazing. Angels are amazing. Yes, I took a picture.

Found a Dime

October 19, 2019

It was a pretty day, so we decided to go fishing, and we were talking about the spirit world. I cannot remember what it was right now, but I asked my father to give me a sign that he was with me, and oh my god, I saw a dime in the water! No way! I quickly asked Geo, "Did you put that there?" He said he did not and would not play a trick like that on me. It's insane! It's insane how much my father loves me. I am so blessed! I so love you, Dad. Yes, I took a video and a picture.

Raven Knocking

October 20, 2019

As we are lying in bed, I heard what sounds like a knocking noise. Geo heard it too. I got out of bed and looked out the front window—nothing… I walked over to the bedroom door and opened it to see if Cody's bedroom door was closed and it was; he is still asleep. I then proceeded to go use the bathroom. I sit down, and I pulled up the shade up to see what the day looks like. As the shade went up, a black raven flies off the ledge and the knocking stops… The last time that happened a secret was revealed to me.

Signs of Az and a Dime

October 21, 2019

As I started my day walking into work, there I saw the word *phoenix* written on the door of the tracker trailer. It's a sign for me, amen. As I walked into the building, I see the driver of the truck, and he also has the word *phoenix* on his company shirt, not all drivers wear their company shirts. I then walk to the front of the club to go punch in for the day, and what do I see? A dime, my father is visiting me. Amen.

A Message from the Spirit World

October 23, 2019

As I was driving home, I received a message from up above. I see a white pick-up truck with the words "Your next move will be the best move" ("jeppi" was written on the back of the truck).

U-Haul

October 29, 2019

As I was driving to work, I saw a broken-down U-Haul truck on the side of the beltway. They all have Arizona plates, so every time I see one, I think of my future home, and it makes me smile. I finally arrive to work, park my car, and start walking in, and I see that there is another U-Haul truck in our receiving area. Signs are everywhere; the angels are amazing. Yes, I took a picture.

Find a Dime

October 30, 2019

Heading to my doctor's appointment to get my varicose veins looked at, my doctor recommended it. I only have health insurance for two more months, so I might as well. I am super early for my appointment, and I am thirsty so I decided to go to Wawa to get a frappe.

As I walked up to pick up my frappe, I see a dime on the floor, and I know that everything will be okay at the doctor's visit. Thank you, Dad, I love you. Yes, I took a picture.

Grateful

November 1, 2019

I was leaving work with a cart full of groceries as I walked past a license plate in the parking lot that read "grateful," and the first thing I thought of was Terry. I am grateful that Terry is my friend. I was going to take a picture of it and send it to her, but because I was leaving later than usual, and I was in a hurry to get home because I had to feed my sick cat with a syringe because he would not eat on his own I did not stop and take a picture. I put my groceries in the trunk and drove off the parking lot. I pulled up to the first traffic light, which is red, and there in front of me is the same car with the license plate "grateful." I knew it was a sign for me to tell her, I am grateful for her, and yes, I took a picture.

Nolan Lane

November 6, 2019

Been chatting with Arizona Bill all afternoon. I always get very happy when I hear from him because he is in my favorite state. I am on cloud nine, happy, happy, happy; it's a natural high for me. This evening, I'm going to have dinner with my son Cody. I'm meeting him there. I Google the directions, which took me a different way, but it's okay it's the scenic way. I liked the ride so much that I decided to take the same way home. As I'm driving home, I see a street sign that reads "Nolan," that's Bill's last name. I cannot make this stuff up; angels were listening to us as we spoke all afternoon about Arizona, they know. I quickly texted Bill and sent him a picture; he was in disbelief. Angels are amazing!

Heart Shape on Roscoe

November 7, 2019

I rushed home to feed my cat Roscoe. He knows the drill. I pick him up, wrap him up in a towel so he will not move, and I feed him with a syringe; he gets goat milk and a high-protein meal. As I am feeding him, Geo texted me that he is on break. I cannot talk right now because I am feeding Roscoe so I take a picture of Roscoe and texted him, "I cannot talk right now, feeding Roscoe." He texted me back, "Look at Roscoe's face. He has a heart-shaped mark on his face." After I finished feeding Roscoe, I read the message and looked at the picture. Oh my god, he does, he does. Awww…I text Geo if he put that there when he released the pressure from the cyst that Roscoe had on his head, and he said, "No, the cut was on top of his head." Is that a sign that Roscoe loves me? Yes, it's a sign. Yes, I took a picture.

???Skywalk, Arizona

November 8, 2019

I went to a mom-and-pop shop to get Roscoe goats milk. The young girl at the counter was having trouble with the register and could not ring me up. Something also about the register tape not cooperating. I was in a hurry because I knew Roscoe would not eat unless I force-fed him I told her I did not need the receipt, but she said she still could not ring me up without the paper in it. She then started making calls, four minutes in now I was getting a little agitated and hot because my cat needed to eat. I liked her shirt but never really paid attention to it, it read "skywalk" on it. Then it dawned on me. Oh my god, that's the Grand Canyon in Arizona! I asked her, "Is that the glass horseshoe walk?" She said yes! I asked her if I could take a picture of her shirt, and she also showed me pictures off her phone while she was waiting for her manager to call her back about the register situation. And it totally turned my unhappy mood to happy mood. I believe this was a sign because if the register tape never ran out I probably would not have noticed her shirt. I thank you, angels. This is another sign that I am going to Arizona.

"It's about to Come to an End"

November 9, 2019

I woke up from a dream; angels sent me a message. I heard them say, "It's about to come to an end." I know they are speaking of Roscoe; they are preparing me for the end. It will still be hard, but I know God is in charge of everything in the universe. I also believe in the spirit leaving the soul, and then it goes to heaven.

Two Dimes, Raven Sings, Roscoe Passes

November 14, 2019

Coming into work this morning, I found two dimes almost back-to-back. Later in that afternoon, I heard a raven calling. I opened up the receiving door to see where he was at; he is on the roof, and as soon as we made eye contact, he stopped and stared at me in silence. Got home late, fed Roscoe, and an hour later, he had passed. I was devastated and crying, but I quickly remembered what the angels had told me five days earlier. I knew Roscoe was going to heaven; my heart is so broken, and as I'm writing this two months later, I am in tears and still emotional. I love you, Roscoe, a furry member of our family forever. Amen.

Roscoe Crosses Over

November 15, 2019

I went to work as usual, but heart is broken. As I am walking across the parking lot, I find a dime, my father's with me. Angel 44 is also around me; they know I am heartbroken. Then around 10:42 a.m., I stepped outside, and I looked up at the sky, and something told me to take a picture at a certain spot. I pulled out my camera and started snapping a few pictures of the sky. That evening, as I'm looking at the pictures, I saw it! I saw a raven in the sky, and then the next picture is even more; it's a raven carrying a cat on its back, it's ROSCOE with *wings*! I can see his outline with his ears and the mark on his face; he looks as though he was looking sideways! He crossed over! The raven (which my father sent me) has Roscoe in heaven with him. What a peaceful and blessed moment for me. Thank you, Dad, thank you, Lord. Roscoe was a blessing in our lives and now in heaven. Amen.

Pop, Roscoe Responding

November 16, 2019

It has been two days since Roscoe's passing. I am in the kitchen cleaning up, and Geo is in the other room watching TV. I decided to speak to Roscoe. I called him like I did when he was with us in my high-pitched voice. I was just talking to him, and as I did, I heard this loud popping noise. Geo quickly asked what was that noise. I turned around to see what it was and the only thing that I saw was an empty Gatorade bottle on the counter. I knew it was Roscoe communicating with me. I knew that he heard me, and he was responding to me. Another sign that Roscoe has crossed over. I love you, Roscoe. Yes, I took a picture.

Hands in Prayer

November 19, 2019

I was on the receiving dock unloading a truck when I noticed a pair of hands in prayer. I quickly took a picture and something told me to pray. I pointed it out to a coworker who was walking by, and he said the same thing, as did the driver that I was unloading. I told the driver that there was a reason why I saw these hands and that I needed to pray. I said a quick prayer and finished unloading the truck.

Four hours later, I'm getting off from work, and as I am driving home, I decided to call my mother just to check in on her. I spoke to her for a few minutes until my sister called her. My mother has call waiting. She came back on the line and told me my sister is on the other line. I tell her, "Go ahead and talk to her. I will talk to you later." I get the urge to start praying again, so I pray the "Our Father" over and over again. This lasted for twenty minutes or so. I'm about three minutes from home when out of the blue, there was a police officer at the bottom of the road, and he was signaling me to pull over.

He got me; speed limit is 25 mph, and I was doing 40 mph, which is normal on this road; it is all wide open, and it's all downhill. He asked me for license and registration. I handed it over, but I am not happy because I do not want to go to court because we are leaving next month. A few minutes later, he came back with a warning. I thanked him for not giving me a ticket and drove off. Now I knew why I saw the hands in prayer; angels were telling me to pray. I truly believed if I did not pray extra that day, I would have gotten a speeding ticket thank you, angels, for watching over me. Yes, I also took a picture.

Found a Dime

November 20, 2019

As I am in conversation with a driver, he told me his wise grandpa used to say, "Common sense is not common." As we walked into the trailer, there it was a dime; my father was agreeing—hahaha. Yes, I took a picture.

Cracked Windshield

November 20, 2019

Took Interstate 95 home because I wanted to take out money out of my Arizona fund to get rid of the wrinkles on my forehead, and then I would replace it later. I knew I was doing something wrong; I could feel it. As I was driving, I was also listening to my last reading with Terry and BOOM! Out of nowhere, something hit my windshield with such force that the glass came through to the inside of my car, and I knew that was a message from above that I should not take out any money for my face or anything else. It really scared me, and yes, I took a picture.

Found a Dime

November 20, 2019

At Giant picking up half-and-half creamer and a few other items, and I decided to pick up my lottery tickets here instead of High's (my regular place). As I'm walking toward the machine, my bags are becoming way too heavy for me, so I set them down for a minute, and as I looked down, there, I see a dime. This was the third dime I saw today. Love you, Dad.

Angel at Repair Shop

November 22, 2019

I am at Safelite about to enter the building to get my windshield repair. I head inside, check in, and then decided to take a walk in nature while I am waiting for the car. I looked up to walk outside, and I saw a white Jeep with license plate 444, and I know it's the angels watching over me. It made me feel good inside. I started walking, and it felt colder than I thought, and I cannot decide if I should return to my car and get my jacket out or not.

Finally, I gave in. I am only seven minutes into my walk so I turn around. I am now at the shop, and my car is already in the bay. I asked if I can retrieve my jacket and the man behind the counter said yes. I walked into the bay and grabbed my jacket; the man that is about to work on my car says, "You can exit from that door," and he pointed to another door. I thank him and proceed to exit. As I exited the building, I saw another license plate with 44 and another license plate with 444 on an actual Safelite van! I know the angels are all around me. Thank you, angels. Yes, I took a picture.

Raven in Mirror

December 3, 2019

I just finished taking a shower, and I pulled back the shower curtains, and I thought I see a raven on the mirror. It's like the whole mirror had steam from me taking a shower except for one part that was in the shape of a raven. I was actually scared and called Geo and asked him if he had cleaned the mirrors before he left for the day, and he said no. I then thought it's my father sending me a message from heaven. Yes, I took a picture.

Found a Dime

December 11, 2019

It's my birthday! We are leaving the house to pick up my two grandsons and my mother; we are going to Taco Bravo for dinner. I walked out to get into Geo's car, which is parked on the street and there was a dime. My father is wishing me happy birthday. Yes, I took a picture.

A House Sign

December 18, 2019

I just pulled up to the High's store to purchase my weekly lottery tickets. I get out of my car, and I see a magnet shaped as a house right next to my feet. I know that this is a sign from my father and above. The day before I had an amazing reading (as usual). One of my cards that was chosen for me read as follows: a happy move to a new home or place of employment is in the works. I knew this was a sign that I was going to have a new house in Arizona. I quickly said a prayer to my beautiful father and the angels and went in to get my lottery tickets. Yes, I took a picture.

Found a Dime

December 21, 2019

It's my sister's birthday! At the casino sitting across from Geo, he told me to pull up closer. I turned to the right to pull up my chair and there between the two tables is a shiny dime; my father is here. I love you, Dad; he sends me a dime for everyone's birthday. In my heart, I felt it's a way of him still connecting with us from heaven. Yes, I took a picture.

Roscoe Visits from Heaven

December 22, 2019

We get into bed and pull the covers up as we snuggled, and I felt a gentle pressure at the bottom of my feet as if someone just sat down, and I knew in an instant it was Roscoe. I was so excited. I quickly said to Geo, "Did you feel that pressure on the bed?" I patted the bed to acknowledge him. I felt the pressure again this time further up the bed toward me. I was so happy, and my heart full of love for Roscoe was with us in spirit. Thank you, Jesus.

Roscoe Visits Again...

December 23, 2019

Roscoe came up on the bed again, I tapped on the bed and called his name in my high-pitched voice, and minutes later, I can feel the pressure of him as he walked across the bed toward me. I love you, Roscoe, spirit world is amazing.

Found a Dime and a Penny

December 26, 2019

Leaving mom's house after the Christmas celebration was over, and it is after midnight. We got to get ice before going home; 7-Eleven is out of ice so we had to go to Royal Farms. They have double doors to enter their store. As I entered the first door, I saw an employee that I always speak with, and we said our hellos, and he said I have not seen you in a while. As I was answering him, I pulled the next door open to enter the building, and as I did, a very shiny object catches my eye so I look down, and in the very end of the door seam, I saw a dime! It's my father sending me a message of Merry Christmas, and he is happy that I went to see my mom who was alone today.

While I was in the store, I could see a spirit floating around in the room; moments later, I see a very shiny penny under the counter, and I know it's Penelope. She is here too! I am so very happy. My phone was in the car, so I took a picture when I got back into the car. I love spirit world. Amen.

Roscoe Again Visits

December 26, 2019

I feel Roscoe on the bed again, so I lay in the opposite direction and started petting him as if he was there in the flesh. I then get up to use the bathroom and then come back to bed; it's 12:59 a.m. I lay in bed and fell asleep and the dream begins…

Roscoe was in midair, floating in slow mode; he was faint looking like a spirit, but strong enough coming through that I could see him. I am cradling him like a baby. The only thing that is different is that his mark on his face is missing. Thank you, Roscoe, for that act of love. Amen.

Dad Surprises Me

January 7, 2020

I am home alone, lying in bed without any thoughts in my head, looking through my phone and then trying to call Priscilla to look for a product for me with no answer. I then go to send her a picture of the product through text, but before I do, a picture of my father popped up all by itself. Oh my God, this has never happened to me before, so I know my father is trying to communicate with me. I just cannot hear him. I started to tell him about my situation and that I need Geo financially right now to get started on my journey out west. I then get this urge to start packing up everything. Thank you, Dad, for loving me so much that you reached out through spirit world to communicate with me. I love you.

Angel 444

January 15, 2020

I am meeting an ex-manager and friend at the doughnut shop to hang out and just chat. She wanted to see me one more time before I moved out west. I pulled into the parking lot, and I saw Angel 444 is here; I got so excited, and I took a picture and my first thought was, *I wonder if this is my friend's new vehicle?* I also see that it is a burnt orange, my second favorite color. This is the same woman that told me about her finding dimes when her mother first passed many years ago. I am so happy to see her and catch up. It's been a while; three hours later, we were done chatting, and we said our goodbyes; we walked outside, and I walked her to her car and it was the burnt orange vehicle with Angel 444 on it. She is an angel to me. Yes, I took a picture.

Angel Appears

January 19, 2020

I love to pray outside while I walk in nature because I feel a stronger connection to the spirit world. I had just finished my prayers, and I was about to text a friend of mine when my phone went from 20 percent charge to nothing at all and it turned itself off; that was odd. That never happened to me before. At first, I was upset, but then I thought to myself I was not supposed to be on the phone at that moment and continued on my way back home, which was now only about nine minutes away, and I would text him when I got home.

I took a few more steps, and that's when I saw her, a beautiful water silhouette of a young child angel in prayer on the sidewalk. She looked so precious and innocent; my first thought was if I was on the phone texting, I would probably have not seen this image, and I was supposed to see her. Angels are amazing. I tried my phone again to see if it would work and it turned on. I could not explain it, but I was able to take a picture. It then turned off again. Minutes later, as I was walking up my cul-de-sac, the phone turned on by itself, and it had again a 20 percent charge left. I cannot make this stuff up. Amen.

Baby Is Coming

January 20, 2020

Priscilla called me and said she is in the hospital. I quickly got dressed and head out for the hospital. Angel 444 was right in front of me. I arrived at the hospital to see my daughter. I could not stay very long because I have an appointment to see the doctor from the other insurance company to evaluate me. I am not very happy about it; this matter should have been resolved earlier (accident from 2017), and my daughter is much more important. Geo then drove me to the doctor's office, which is clearly across town. I am so upset and then I see Angel 444 again, and I know everything will be okay. I quickly texted Terry to tell her what is going on, and then I thought of what she had taught me. "I was not supposed to be there at that moment." I have my visit with the doctor, only a few minutes in length. We then left and proceeded to head back, and I saw Angel 444 once more, and I know that everything will fall into its right place. Thank you, angels. Yes, I took pictures.

Baby Arrives

January 20, 2020

Baby Dino arrives! Both mom and baby are fine. I get to hold him and take a few pictures of this special moment. I, again, cannot stay very long because I am watching my older two grandsons while mommy is with her new baby. I said my goodbyes and proceeded to go home as I'm walking to my car, I see a license plate that reads "grm grm" (short for grandma), and I automatically know it's a sign from above. I am being congratulated on being a grandma from my father and the angels. I pull away, and on my way home, Angel 44 is in front of me confirming this. Yes, I took a picture; angels are amazing. Thank you.

Visit Dad before Leaving for Arizona

January 29, 2020

I want to see my father one last time before my big journey out west starts. I asked my mother to come along. We arrived at the cemetery; it is *cold*. We both get out of the car to say our prayers, and then my mother returned quickly to the car. As I am finishing up my prayers. I see a low-flying plane; it's a Southwest plane, and a raven flying in the same direction, followed by a cloud shaped as a raven, and I knew my father was also saying goodbye, but at the same time, he was telling me that he would follow me out there. My dad is an amazing man, father, and angel. I love you, Dad. Yes, I took pictures.

Jesus Dream/Savannah

January 29, 2020

I had a dream about Jesus; it seemed so surreal. "To dream of Jesus is a sign of strength and satisfaction. This dream indicates to be happy as your life will be joyful and peaceful." I had another dream that same night in which I saw the word SAVANNAH. It suggested that you need to learn to adjust the various situations and circumstances. Appreciate the different experiences in your life even though they are not what you may be accustomed too. Both of these dreams were sent to me from spirit world to prepare me on my journey that I was going to embark on. My journey started four days later on February 2, 2020.

Spirit Knocking

February 4, 2020

It's the 3:00 a.m. hour in Alabama, and I'm sleeping when I hear a knocking on our walls; it awakes me, and I check around and no one is there. It's peaceful everywhere. Was I dreaming, or was it spirit, trying to get my attention? I looked up spiritual meaning of knocking: "You may have a spirit on your hands." "Some believe a knocking spirit is asking for entry in your home, which would only lead to a more entrenched spiritual presence, while other suggest this type of entity just wants to get your attention." I then fell back asleep.

Ladybug Visits Make a Wish...

February 4, 2020

Geo and I are about to start our third day of driving. He opened the front door of our hotel room, and there on the door is a ladybug. A sign of good luck. I told him we have to make a wish! What a beautiful way to start the day. Yes, I took a picture, and I made a wish.

Found a Dime

February 4, 2020

Third day of our journey, and I am in the state of Alabama! Beautiful people! Beautiful scenery. As I'm talking to the wonderful lady behind the counter at the Wingate hotel to check out. I see a dime on the floor in the lobby hallway to my right. It's 8:28 a.m., and the lobby is empty. I know that my father is here. I'm so excited that he is on this journey with me. It makes my heart smile. I told the wonderful lady behind the counter of how I find dimes everywhere! It's a message of love from my father. Yes, I took a picture.

Arizona Tags in New Orleans

February 4, 2020

We are in New Orleans, and it is really raining hard. I am so frustrated! It's hard when you're driving in the area that you're not familiar with; visibility is low, it gets dark earlier, it's around rush-hour traffic time, and everyone is going way too fast! As I'm driving, a black car in the distance caught my eye even though it is blending in with the dark evening skies, and then see it: Arizona license plates. I know that the angels, spirit world, and my beautiful father are telling me of my goal of reaching Arizona. All the frustration went away, and I am in my happy place once again. Thank you, angels. I love you, angels.

Found a Dime

February 4, 2020

New Orleans, French Quarter, Bourbon Street, what a beautiful way to end the evening! We walk the streets of Bourbon; this is where Mardi Gras is held every year. They were having preparties. We saw many sites, great music, great people, gift shops, and even had a great dinner with dessert too. I even got to dance and got my first set of beads! What an evening. We now begin to walk to our car to get some well-needed sleep to continue our journey out west. We were walking in a dark alley, and I feel a little scared because we are away from people, and we're in an unknown place. Minutes later, something shiny caught my eye, and I walked up to it. It's a dime! I quickly became not afraid anymore; my father is with us. I'm so happy I love him so much thanks for watching over us. Yes, I took a picture.

Angels Lead the Way

February 6, 2020

I am getting so excited; every day we get closer to your goal of Arizona! We are driving seven to eight hours a day. As we are on the road, I can see Arizona tags again, which make my heart smile. Angels are leading the way, amen. Yes, I took a picture.

Angel 444-4444

February 7, 2020

"Everything is bigger in Texas." We have been driving for two long days, and we are still in the great state of Texas. As I'm driving, I see Angel 444-4444. It is on a billboard so *huge* I couldn't miss it, and I knew the angels were with me. I am so blessed; words cannot express the love. Yes, I took a picture.

Pickup Truck 44

February 7, 2020

Geo wanted to stop in a little town called Bandera, Texas. He wanted to see a real cowboy town and at the same time have lunch. We split a cheesesteak, and off we went to explore the town. As we are walking around, I see a black pickup truck with 44 on it. I get so happy that the angels are with me on this beautiful journey in my life. As we continued to walk, Geo saw an old-time wild, wild west saloon like they had in the western movies; it had the saloon doors and even a hitching rail for the horses! Geo said, "Let's go in and have a drink with some real cowboys." We entered the saloon and see real cowboys drinking beer. Geo introduced us and said that I always wanted to have a drink with real cowboys. We sat down, and Geo insisted on buying a round of beers for everyone and a water for me. We have been there now for hours and hours, laughing, talking, and joking around, and having the best time ever. Texas has some *true, real cowboys, amen.*

Before we know it, it was evening time, dinnertime. I've always heard Texas has the best steak, and that's what I wanted to eat. They recommended a steak place a few blocks down, and then we were going to meet up again at a different saloon. We could not find the other saloon, so we decided to go back to the original saloon where we first met them to see if they were still there, and they were there and very much drunk too. They finished up their last beer, and we were going to follow them to the next saloon. As we walked outside and proceeded to the vehicles, I noticed that one of the cowboys was walking up to the same exact black pickup truck that I saw way earlier in the daytime with the license plate 44 on it; oh my God, he was a very kind cowboy who offered us (two complete strangers) a free place for the night. What a good soul; God bless him. Earlier in the day, I thought to myself, *I wonder if that is his pickup truck?*

Angels are amazing. We were supposed to meet these kind souls. Yes, I took a picture.

Found a Dime

February 8, 2020

What a night! I was serenaded all evening by a cowboy with his magic guitar. What a special moment in time. I will never forget; it was so beautiful. We we're in between the kitchen (which has a breakfast bar loop around it) and the living room. I got up to stretch my legs, and on the breakfast bar, I saw a dime! My father is here. My father was here. I love him so much. I am so blessed to have a father who loves me so much. Yes, I took a picture. I did not notice it most of the evening and into the early hours of the morning because there were so many different objects on the breakfast bar at the time. I was so excited I had to tell them the story behind the dimes. Jerry, the owner of the house, was such a good man; he said I could take it. I did not want to take it without replacing it with another one. I gave him a quarter. It was a perfect evening to a perfect day. Thank you, Lord.

A Very Special Feather

February 8, 2020

Been driving all day, and it's the last fill up before we hit the next stop. Last fill up before we hit the next state, and one last chance to find something special that represents what Texas means to me. As we are filling up both cars, we walked into the convenient shop for a snack and some water. I wanted to look around the store as a one more time to see if I see anything that catches my attention, and then I saw it! A feather with a Texas flag on it. I knew it was a spiritual message from above. I met two angels in Texas, Jerry and Kevin, and all their friends took us in and made us feel welcome and even provided a place to rest and a warm meal the following morning. Two angels forever in my heart. Yes, I took a picture, and I bought it.

Angel Key No. 4

February 8, 2020

We have been driving *all day long*; it is evening time now, so we are going to grab a bite to eat and get some sleep so we can do it all over again tomorrow. We drive around, looking for a motel nearby and calling to check prices. Finally we find one that is reasonable. I go in to check in and receive my key. Oh my god, it's angel #4! I'm so blessed and so excited that I immediately run over to Geo to show him. Angels are again confirming that they are with us as we journey out west to find our new home. Yes, I took a picture.

Find a Dime

February 9, 2020

We are in Roswell, New Mexico, and lately, I have been craving steak tacos! We stop and have a bite to eat here because Geo tells me that Roswell is where the aliens landed. After lunch, we start to walk around and check out the sights, it is a windy day, but the sky is beautiful; I tell my father in prayer I wish he was here to see the beauty, and if he was not too busy to visit me and send me a sign. As we walked a few blocks higher, I see a dime! My father is here; my father is here. I quickly tell Geo what I asked of my dad, and he showed up! Geo saw it also as I walked up to it and he took a picture of the dime and myself. Thank you, Dad. I love you, Dad.

Alien in the Sky

February 9, 2020

As we are driving through Roswell, I even see what looks like an alien in the sky! Yes, I took a picture.

A sign from My Father...Raven

February 9, 2020

Driving to Arizona; we are so very close. I'm so excited! I start to pray to God and thank him. I am so emotional I am crying with joy. I want make the world a better place. Thoughts were pouring in faster than I could write them down. I then started talking to my dad; I told him how much I loved him, and I am happy that he is with me. I have tears of joy is running down my face. As I am talking to him in prayer, I saw a large raven start to appear in the sky with its feathers spread out, and I knew my father heard me talking to him. I love you, Dad. Yes, I took a picture.

Seeing a Piece of the Rainbow

February 10, 2020

We are only a short distance from a place I will call home, ARIZONA! We make one last stop at a little shop so I could pick up a souvenir from the beautiful state of New Mexico. As we exit the building, Geo noticed a small rainbow that is touching the ground. I am moved to tears. I get on my knees and thank God, the angels, my father, and the spirit world for this blessing. My journey home is near. I even see a rabbit (spiritual meaning of rabbit a symbol of prosperity abundance fertility and a new life). Amen.

Entering Rainbow: Arrived in Arizona

February 10, 2020

We get into our cars and start driving again… I am so excited at this point we are so close! I keep looking in my rearview mirror. I know I'm going to see a full rainbow in the sky behind me; it is really dark, and it is slightly drizzling. The sun is in front of us peeking through the clouds, and there it is a *rainbow*. One of the *biggest ones* I had ever seen! I quickly pulled over, got out my car, and took a video of God's breathtaking creation, *beautiful*. I was speechless. My first thought was of my son, Angelo, who visited Arizona the year before while working; he was here for three days, and he kept saying that it was raining. I could not believe it; it never rains there.

On the third day, the day he was leaving he said he saw the *biggest rainbow ever*! At that moment, I thought of my father, I told Angelo that was a sign from my father that he is going to live in Arizona with me. God and his angels were letting me know through spirit world that I was at the end of the rainbow. I made it. I was finally here…I was home… Amen…

Dream of Father

February 12, 2020

First night in California, I wake up to a very loving dream… I dream of my father sending me repeated rainbows over and over and over… Spiritual meaning of rainbow: Dreaming of a rainbow is a sign of good luck, prosperity, hope, and success. A rainbow represents a bridge between your earthly and higher selves. These are spiritual bridges you cannot physically cross to reach the pot of gold. This can be the time where you may have many creative ideas and you enjoy life to the fullest.

Angel on Stone

February 12, 2020

We start to get hungry and want to take a break from driving; we see these outlets from in the distance and decide to stop there. Wow, what a really nice establishment. As we are walking and taking in the sights, I cannot help but notice a stone that has an angel on it with its wings spread out. I am so happy that spirit world is around me. I can clearly see the angel and call Terry right away. I have to show her this beauty of a rock. God and his angels are truly amazing, and they are everywhere. Yes, I took a picture.

Found a Dime

February 13, 2020

I asked my father to visit me if he had a minute this evening; we were having dinner in San Francisco. As we finished dinner, I walked up to the counter to ask a question I had about the delicious dinner that Geo had and there right in front of me as I looked down was a dime! I quickly picked it up and went to show Geo! Yes, I took a picture. I love you, Dad!

Raven on License Plate

February 14, 2020

We are leaving the marina and started driving again when this silver car gets in front of us and started driving crazy. The license plate caught my eye. Oh my god, it read, "RAVEN ON." I know that is a message from my beautiful father! It's our first Valentine's Day on the west coast, and what a special way to remember it. I can feel his love. Geo cannot explain it! Yes, I took a picture.

Angel 44 at Hollywood Sign

February 16, 2020

California sightseeing: I told Geo I like to see the "Hollywood" sign. I've seen this historic sign for many years in movies, and now that we are in California, I would love to see it live. As we pulled up to Griffith Park and started to pull into an open parking space, I saw Angel 44 directly in front of us! I get so happy. Angels are with us. Yes, I took a picture.

Angel 44 and the Walk of Fame

February 16, 2020

Another landmark I wanted to see is the famous "Walk of Fame." Growing up in the seventies and eighties, I would see it in movies and thought it was the coolest thing. Geo dropped me off so I could walk it (no place to park so Geo just kept circling around). I walked a little section, and I was happy. Geo popped up around the corner at the same time I was ready to jump in the car again. As soon I got into the car, the "city sightseeing" bus jumped in front of us, and Angel 44 is on the license plate. Angels are amazing and always among us. Yes, I took a picture.

Found a Dime

February 20, 2020

Sitting outside for dinner with breathtaking views of the mountains as we are finishing up Mexican steak tacos. Geo started looking for motels again for the evening—"our daily thing." *I want a place to call home and a job.* I'm saying this to myself over and over. As Geo was on his phone, I saw something super shiny on the parking lot. I leaned over in the chair and it disappeared, and then I lean backward, and I see it again. Is it a drop of water? Can it be a dime? I leaned forward and backward a few more times and then decided to get up and get a closer look. As I started taking steps getting closer to it, I noticed it was a dime! My father is here; it made me so happy. I quickly turned to Geo and pointed to the dime. Geo is used to this by now, and did not reply, I picked up the dime and thanked him for being here with me. I asked him to help us with our money situation and a place for the evening; the motels are draining us. Yes, I took a picture. Thank you, Dad, I love you.

Book Cover and Name

February 23, 2020

I woke up to a dream that was so vivid about my book and what colors to use and what to name it. It was also put in my head an idea that I should have two books instead of just one. One would be called "FIND A DIME" blue cover with a dime in the center and in white large letters; I could see it in my dream: FIND. A. DIME.

Second one will have two angels in the shape of the number 7 because I mostly see angels from the right side and reminds me of the number 7. I then woke up and quickly wrote it down. It's funny we are staying at an Airbnb and our blanket is the shade of blue, which I saw in my dreams. Angels are amazing.

Home at 444

February 27, 2020

We have been searching for a place to call home. The first place was nice on the inside and had the perfect view of the sun setting over the mountain, but we did not feel safe. The second place was even nicer but smaller, and we were denied because of bad credit/low score. I filed bankruptcy two years earlier because of a relationship breakup involving a house that I cannot afford on my own and tried to sell it before I was in the red, but it did not happen in time. Simply, it was not meant for this to be our home. Geo was disappointed and asked the obvious question that if they denied us, then everyone else would deny us for the same reason, which would be a waste of time and what would he recommend for us? The man recommended us to Valley King properties and gave us their number and their address. We called and an angel by the name of Ashley picked up the phone and scheduled us to meet with her at 1:00 p.m. if that worked good for us, which it did.

We were only twenty minutes away from her. We arrived and were quickly greeted by this very beautiful and kind woman. We told her who we were and that we had an appointment with Ashley; she responded by saying she was Ashley, and if we could start filling out some paperwork for her, she would be right with us. Minutes later, she walked over and called us back. She was so very kind and explain what this company did to help people. It is a free apartment locating and home sales, which helped people with good/bad credit and people who are relocating from another state that need help finding a home.

She asked us some questions and then ran a credit report on us. She said our credit was not that bad, only two things were showing on mine, but everything else was dismissed in the bankruptcy. She asked what we were looking for in an apartment and then started making phone calls. She set us up to meet with Robin to look at an apartment. She looked at us and said that she found a place that we would really be happy with and to call her after we went to see it and tell her what we thought. She gave Geo the address, and we proceeded to drive there to check it out. It is only sixteen minutes away. OH MY GOD! As we are pulling up into the place, I see Angel 444! Oh my god, I start to cry!

Oh my God! I told Geo, "Why didn't you tell me the address?"

His reply was he wanted to surprise me. Angels are *amazing*! Ashley is an angel and amazing. I had to take a picture and quickly send it to Terry! (My beautiful friend, and psychic/medium also.) I was so overjoyed and very emotional, and I wanted to say a prayer to God and the angels. THANK YOU, THANK YOU, THANK YOU, THANK YOU. I cannot make this stuff up!

I quickly called Ashley and got voicemail, and I repeatedly thanked her. We went inside and met with Robin; we had to fill out more paperwork, and we're given information about the apartment. Two units were available, but we were only to see one at the moment because the other one was not available for show because it was being remodeled. As we were being shown the unit, I saw that there were two angels ornament hanging nearby, and I knew that was another sign. When we returned to the office, Geo started finishing up the paperwork as I asked for the address location of the other unit to see where it was located. I went over to check it out; it was set back away from the street and had a breathtaking view in the backyard of a large pond with lots of nature surrounding it and incredible view of the sun as it was setting. In the front, I saw angels everywhere on the unit below and to the left of the unit, I was looking at. There was an old woman sitting there, and I told her we were looking at two apartments and they both had angels near them and that I was very spiritual, so she asked, "Which has more angels?"

I replied, "Yours, first apartment has two, you have eight."

I quickly ran to the leasing office and told Geo I wanted the unit I just went to see from the outside only. HOME SWEET HOME, thank you, Angel 444. We received our key on February 29, 2020.

Our new address is 444 N. Gila Springs Blvd., Chandler, Arizona, 85226, unit 2049.

Penelope Visits Our New Place

March 1, 2020

Our first full day at our new home; as we are outdoors enjoying the warm weather, we are greeted by the beautiful Penelope in the sky (she is one of my spirit guides who always wears a long dress and she reminds me of a señorita). I am so grateful that she is with us. Thank you, Penelope! Yes, I took a picture.

Angel 44 at AZ DOT

March 5, 2020

I'm so excited. Geo is taking me to get my new Arizona driver's license today! We pulled up into the parking lot, and there is Angel 44! I am so happy angels are with me! I get my temporary paper license and my real license will be mailed to me. Yes, I took a picture.

Vision of Mary

April 3, 2020

We climbed to the top of a small mountain, and the view is breath-taking. I am at such peace within my soul that I feel the urge to pray. I also want to thank God for Mother Earth and to have the sight to see it all. I also say a prayer for all who have crossed over because of the coronavirus that is upon the world now. As I was praying, I am admiring the beauty of the world when I see the Virgin Mary appear on the side of the mountain she has her veil on and is holding up two fingers as if she is giving me the peace sign. I feel she is telling me that everything will be okay. Then the sun went behind the clouds, and the vision disappeared and then the sun came out from behind the clouds, and I could see her again. I quickly called Geo over to witness this miracle; he can see something, but he's not sure what it is. I quickly take a picture. I called my mother the next day and sent a picture, but both my mother and brother cannot see it. Maybe the vision was only meant for me to see. Bless the Almighty. Amen, amen.

Found a Dime

April 5, 2020

Went to California for the ride so Geo could get some goodies for himself. I waited in the car. I do not believe in that stuff, and I do not feel comfortable in there. I felt scared while waiting for him. Geo finally came out, and we left, and of course, I have to empty out my bladder. I asked him to stop by the Rite Aid, which was right up the street so I could use the bathroom. I felt worried and scared because as I entered the store almost everyone had a mask on. I quickly went to use the bathroom and got out of there right away.

As I stepped outside and started to walk to the car, I saw an old man with a guitar starting to play. It felt so good and peaceful. I went to the car and asked Geo if I could give him change. Geo gave me two dollars and told me, "Don't hug him because of what is going on in the world." As I approach the very dark-skinned man he reminded me of my father; he was just as dark as my father, and the more I looked at him, the more he resembled my father. I did not want to stare too much because one of his eyes was completely out of his eye socket, and I did not want him to feel uncomfortable. I kept thinking of my father; I gave him the two dollars and thanked him for playing he replied, "God bless you."

He had a little dog, which I asked him about, and as he began to speak, I noticed a dime on the sidewalk. My father, my father was here. I quickly walked over and picked up the dime and explain to the man how my father always sends me dimes from heaven. Did I find a dime because I felt scared earlier of where we were at or because everyone had a mask on or because this beautiful man looked and reminded me of my father (a sign of protection)? I then said my goodbyes and jumped in the car and took a picture of the dime; phone was in the car.

I love you, Dad.

Help with Publishing Book Answered

April 6, 2020

In prayer, I asked for help with publishing my book; well, that evening, while we were watching the television, a commercial came on. It was a publishing company, and they were offering a free kit to help one get started, myfreeauthorkit.com. Angels are amazing.

First Easter

April 12, 2020

I'm outside writing my book; as I am writing I have to go back and forth to see the picture of my entry. As I am doing this the catalog of people and faces comes up all on its own, and I see my father's picture and it makes me smile. Then out of nowhere, a picture of him holding a big glass and giving a toast comes up all by itself, and I know it's him saying "Buona Pasqua" (Happy Easter). It's my first Easter away from family. I love him so much he made my first Easter out west perfect!

Angel 44 at AZ DOT Again

April 16, 2020

I'm so excited, I am pulling into the Arizona Department of Transportation parking lot to go get my Arizona tags for my car! As I pull in there, Angel 44 is already there and waiting. I'm so happy, angels are with me. One hour later, I got my tags! My car is now official! Yes, I took a picture. Angels are amazing!

Spirit Knocking

April 19, 2020

Hear, a light tapping on the wall over and over again; it sounds so real I get up to go check the peephole. Some nights Geo hears it also. This has been happening for a while now. In my April reading with Terry, she asked have I been hearing knocking on the walls. It's my father; he wants me to be happy. My father is amazing! "Faith comes from hearing and hearing by the word of God," "When you hear a knock you can respond, it means you are qualified to open the door to whatever God wants from or for you." Amen…

Found Elephant

April 24, 2020

In my last reading, Terry said to get an elephant with its trunk up and place it in a room of the front of the house facing the same direction; it brings in money. She said it could be a picture or a statue; it did not matter. My father had told her to tell me this. My aunt had one in her home when we were growing up, and she always had good luck. So now I was on the hunt. I have been looking for days at different stores. Eight days later, I am at Michael's arts and craft store when I come to the clearance section, and there on the shelf it is! A small, silver elephant with its trunk way up! I pick it up and look it over as this song is playing over head in the store. At first, I do not pay attention to it, but then, the words kept playing over and over and over again saying, "I found you, I found you." I quickly get out my phone to "Shazam" it to see the name and artist of the song. Oh my god, oh my god, oh my god; it's called "I Found You" by Benny Blanco and Calvin Harris. I know it's a message from my father and spirit world; that this is the elephant! Spirit world is amazing! My father is amazing! I purchased it, and it is in the front of our home facing the front! Yes, I took a picture. THANK YOU, DAD.

Gifted Elephant

April 30, 2020

Out walking and talking to Paul; I had to tell him about my elephant story. He was totally in awe with it. Now it is four days later... After three hours of walking, I am home when there is a knock on the door. I opened the door and there on the ground is a package addressed to me from Paul. I got excited, grabbed a knife, sat on the couch next to Geo, and called Paul before I begin to open it. OMG! It's an elephant with its trunk up! I am so deeply touched by this act of kindness and love. Geo is also impressed. I love it. I express my thankfulness to Paul. What a beautiful elephant, and now I have two. I placed it on the end table facing the front of the house beautiful. I love you, Paul. Geo captures the moment with a picture of me holding the elephant.

God is amazing; friends are amazing.

A Mother's Day Gift of Love

May 4, 2020

Happy birthday, Mom! First birthday ever I will not be able to see my mother on her birthday. :(Geo and I spent the whole day out. Evening time, we arrive at the apartment; it's Geo's turn to get the mail. Geo has a package that is addressed to me! I'm excited, who is it from, and what's in it? It's from Vanessa! I cannot wait I have to open it now! I opened the package, and my emotions started to show it's a bracelet with a dime on it and the card reads, "Mommy, Happy Mother's Day! Now you can have your father with you everywhere!"

It was the most moving gift equal to giving birth to my children. I was so emotional and in tears my heart was moved so much, and I had such joy and love within it. What a beautiful gift and to receive it on my mother's birthday was even more special to me. Geo was so touched himself; he has been giving and receiving gifts for over forty years and has never experienced a gift like that. Thank you, Vanessa. I love you with *all my heart*. Yes, I took a picture.

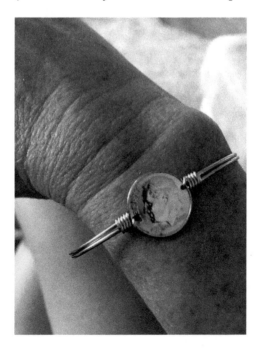

Angel 44 Calls

May 8, 2020

Lately, every day after my walk, I go sit on the picnic table behind our apartments, and I write in my journal until the phone is depleted of juice. I've been writing for over an hour when my phone rang. I normally would not answer it, but something told me to answer it. It is the publishing company that I contacted about a month ago to send me their free package on how to publish a book, and I had some questions for him which he answered; we spoke for twenty minutes. After we hung up, I realized that the last two digits of the phone number were 44!

Angels are amazing: (646) 214-7044.

"I Love You" Dream

May 9, 2020

I woke up from a dream in which I was told "I love you." It felt so good within my soul. Angels are amazing." When hearing "I love you" in a dream as a beautiful and happy vision that is defined as the presence of God.

God is amazing, amen…

Mother's Day Raven

May 10, 2020

It's my very first Mother's Day in Arizona, and I wanted to spend it in Sedona, where I feel a spiritual connection. It's also my first Mother's Day in which I know that I will not see any of my kids because they all live on the East Coast. As we arrived, there are many people out enjoying the day as well, even though the COVID-19 is still a threat. I am enjoying the warm weather and taking in all the beauty that God has made. We have now spent hours here, and as we are walking, one of the largest ravens I have ever seen flew very low toward me and landed on a perch directly in my path. I know that this is a sign from my father! I am so very excited and emotional. I was so very happy my father has sent me a sign of love and a greeting of Happy Mother's Day to me. God bless him. I love you, Dad. Geo has also witnessed this and he knows, he knows... Yes, I took a picture and a video! God and angels are amazing.

Follow Your Dreams…Rainbow

May 10, 2020

Driving home from Sedona, I want to hear the song "When the Heart Rules the Mind" by GTR. I always feel a connection when I hear this song, and today it gave me goosebumps and chills. I know my father is speaking to me through this song. I love him so much. We are almost home, and Geo saw a rainbow. A rainbow on a sunny day! My father loves me so much, and he knew my first Mother's Day away from my kids would be hard, so he made sure it was a very special one for me. What a special way to end my first Mother's Day. I feel totally loved. Thank you, Dad. Yes, I took a picture.

Found a Dime

May 11, 2020

I wanted to go to Sedona two days in a row—Mother's Day and the day after. I feel such a connection out there. We're going to walk around and have lunch; we decide to go to Chipotle. Geo is not being very nice to me today; it is putting such a strain on this beautiful, beautiful day. We enter Chipotle; it is empty inside, and it is carry out only because of the COVID-19 rules still in effect. Geo is being stubborn and refuses to have lunch with me so I walked up to place my order, and there next to all the empty tables, I see a dime, and I know my father is here with me. He knows Geo is being mean. Seeing the dime made me feel good inside. Thank you, Dad, I needed that. I love you. Yes, I took a picture.

Found a Dime

May 14, 2020

Went to post office to mail eight postcards to my family. As I walked up to the counter, I see a dime. It is slightly hidden in the corner of the wall. I know my father's happy with me sending these postcards out. It will make everyone smile, thanks, Dad. I did not take a picture because my camera was in the car.

Happy Birthday, Conner

May 19, 2020

It's my grandson's birthday today—no. 11! I got up a little later than normal it's 7:30 a.m. here and 10:30 a.m. on the East Coast. I decided to call my grandson before I begin my prayers because I know that he is up by now, and I have the best chance of reaching him. I FaceTime him, and he picked up right away. HAPPY BIRTHDAY, CONNER! He is excited, and we started talking about the events that will take place today. I reached to the end of the parking lot and make a left about ten steps in, I see a green balloon lying on the side of the curve on the street!

I knew right away in my heart my father is sending happy birthday wishes to his great-grandson from heaven. Since I am on FaceTime, I flipped the screen and show my grandson the balloon that his great-grandfather sent him from heaven. Spirit world is amazing; my dad is amazing. I love you, Dad! We then say goodbye, and we hang up. I start my prayers. I'm about fifteen minutes in when I think of my birthday a few years back when I was in Atlantic City, and I saw a balloon half-deflated on the beach that read "HAPPY BIRTHDAY," and I knew it was my father sending birthday wishes to me from heaven. He was repeating this with his great-grandson. As soon as I had this memory, I see a truck parked in the driveway with a license plate that reads "ELE11VN," my grandson's age today. Amen, amen! I know my father is here in spirit. I love him so much. Thank you, Dad. Yes, yes, I took a picture.

Forty-four Times

May 22, 2020

We are in Sedona again today. I cannot get enough of this place; it is breathtaking! As we are coming up to the very end of all the gift shops, I noticed a car parked to my right in front of the very last shop, the tag reads "44 times"—oh my god! I cannot make this stuff up. I'm so excited. Angel 44 is here with us. I need to know the story. Geo circled back around and took forever to find a parking space because of how the town is set up. I keep praying that the car does not leave. Finally, we parked, and I told Geo I will be right back.

I ran up the road, crossed the street, and opened the front door of the gift shop where a woman was looking right at me and the following words just come out of my mouth, "Do you know who owns the car that is parked right up front here is?" I heard a woman's voice say, "It's mine." I looked over to my left, and there behind the counter is an older woman. I quickly explained that Angel 44 is my angel number, and I see it everywhere and if she could explain "44 times." Is it her angel number too? She replied it's something between her husband and her, something like every time they say "I love you" they add forty-four times at the end, and it also has a deeper personal meaning. I quickly thanked her for letting me know, and I leave. Yes, I took a picture. Angels are amazing.

"Take Me Home and Spread Kindness"

May 22, 2020

Geo and I are hiking the mountains of Sedona when I noticed something reflecting off the sun and is catching my attention in a small bush. As I get closer, I noticed a tiny black polka dot feather attached to a chain, which is attached to a white square. At first, I am scared to touch it because Geo always told me about snakes hiding in bushes, but because the feather is a sign for me, I decided to quickly go for it.

OMG, what a message! The white square has a message written on it that reads, "Take me home and spread kindness." Angels are amazing. God is amazing. A black feather also symbolizes protection. Yes, I took a picture, and I took it home with me.

Life-Size Angel

May 23, 2020

I just finished my walk, and I am in the backyard of our apartment complex. The ray of light off the morning sun is a beauty; it sends rays in every direction. In one of my pictures, the sun's rays cast a spotlight on a tree that has a life size angel that is praying in it. Angels are everywhere! God is *amazing*. Yes, I took a picture.

Flat Balloon

May 24, 2020

As I'm walking, I see a single-family home that overlooked a parking garage, and I said to myself, "Why would someone get a single-family home that overlooks a parking garage?"

I want a single-family home that has a view of the sun from the time it comes up to the time it comes down, Lord, with no obstructions. As soon as I say this, I see what looks like a deflated balloon in my path. As I get closer to it, I noticed Angel 444! The Lord and the angels are listening to my prayers, amen. Yes, I took a picture.

Tigger

May 30, 2020

A few days earlier, Julie sent me a picture and a video of her kitten, Tigger. It made me smile, he was such a beauty of a kitten; she also texted me that he was coming up on the anniversary of his passing of June 5 (he passed away from pneumonia). I decided to say a prayer for him. He sent me a special message today from heaven that he had crossed over. I did not see it right away; it was not until the evening time that I was going through my photos of the day, and I noticed a kitten in the clouds. It was Tigger. I could see the features from his face and his body also. God is amazing. He truly, truly is amazing. Amen.

"Then You Found Your Heaven"

June 7, 2020

We are driving home from another lovely day in Sedona. We are halfway home when I noticed a license plate that says "Lina 57"; that's my aunt's name. I'm so happy; never did I ever imagine to see "Lina" on a license plate. It's like winning the lottery! I quickly take a picture and send it to my family group text and then wonder should I send it to my cousin to show her mom (which is my aunt Lina). I'm debating, and then I decide to send it, even if I do not receive a reply back. One minute later, I received a text from my cousin, letting me know that she will show her in the morning because my aunt's already gone to sleep. We start texting back and forth for the first time ever; it was great. In these text exchanges, my cousin said two powerful statements that I felt close to my heart.

First statement was "Just keep the lines of communication open." I know this is very important to me because I am now living over two thousand miles away from my family. I am following my dreams of living in the sun. I love the warm weather, and I am a sun worshiper. Second statement was "Then you have found your heaven." Three minutes later, a yellow Jeep catches my attention; on its spare wheel, the message reads, "ENJOY THE RIDE." I know this is a message from spirit world to me. Thank you, angels. I need to learn how to just sit back and enjoy life. I really do. I am a very stubborn Italian. Yes, I took a picture.

Vanessa Found a Dime

June 12, 2020

Got up super early and started texting with my younger daughter, Vanessa. She told me that she went to get a cup of coffee from the break room, and there on top of the empty cups was a dime. She took a picture to show me. I'm so happy that my father checks in on all my kids (his grandkids). I love him.

A Painting of 44

June 18, 2020

We went to Red Rock Canyon today. What beauty in what God has made. With all the driving and light walking, my eyes are tired; they are still in healing mode from a surgery I had done sixteen days earlier, and they need a break. As we drove back to the hotel, I told Geo that I will head up to the room to rest my eyes for twenty minutes or so. Geo agreed and decided to play slots for a while, so I can have some peace and quiet. He will be up shortly. I get to the room, rinse off, lay in bed, close my eyes, and rest, ahhhhh…

Thirty minutes passed, I opened my eyes; it felt so good to rest them. I decided to stay in bed with my eyes open, and I started looking around the room. I like the quietness, and as I looked at the painting on the wall to my left, I noticed something that I did not notice the day we arrived, which was the day before. Angel 44 is on the painting! I see the number 44 in the painting itself, and I know angels are with me. I am so happy and blessed. Thank you, angels. Yes, I took a picture.

Found an Angel

June 18, 2020

We are at the Flamingo Hotel and Casino, walking around as Geo decided which slot he wanted to play. As we were walking around, I noticed something shiny catch my eye; at first I think it's a dime, and as I go grab for it, I noticed it is not a dime, but an angel. It's an angel pendant! There is an angel on the front and a message in a back that reads, "Watch over me." I feel blessed. Yes, I took a picture. Angels are among us always.

Two Dimes and a Bible Verse

June 20, 2020

We are walking the streets of Vegas and taking in the sights; I found a dime. I am happy my father is here. I keep telling Geo that if my father was here in the flesh, he would love Vegas. As we continued to walk, I found yet another dime; my father heard my comment about him and sent me another dime—it made us both smile. As we continued to walk, I noticed a young man walking toward us. He has a black T-shirt on with a Bible verse number written in white, 4:44, which grabbed my attention right away. Angel 4 is amazing. I could not take a picture because I left the phone in the hotel room.

Rock Angel

June 20, 2020

I love the red rocks of the west, so while we are in Vegas, Geo decided to take me to "Valley of Fire." The creation and beauty that God has made is simply breathtaking. As I stood on a large rock to take pictures of such beauty, I noticed an angel so beautiful it captured my attention. I can see the head and the wing; I quickly pointed it out to Geo, and he could see the angel also. Angels are amazing; they are constantly in our lives. Thank you for such a blessing. Yes, I took a picture.

The Big Push

June 21, 2020

In my prayers this morning, I asked for help with publishing my book. I need a *big push*. I cannot remember the exact words, but I wanted the most forceful force to help me. I want to have it done by the end of this month; it's well overdue. We went to Jimmy Buffet's Margaritaville for breakfast. Geo was doing my unemployment, and he told me, "You must've won your appeal because the dates in question showed up and that means you should be receiving a large lump of money at one time." I became very emotional and started to cry. I then started to hear the song "Three Little Birds" by Bob Marley playing in the background and the video was playing on all the big-screen televisions that were in the room, and I knew at that moment the angels answered my prayers. Now I have the money to publish this book. We then left and there I saw Angel 44 confirming. Yes, I took a picture. As we entered the next casino, I heard the words being sung overhead, "I'll be there to protect and to shelter you," and I knew angels were still around me. The song is called "Reach Out (I'll Be There)" by The Four Tops. An endless day of angels. Amen.

Found a Dime

July 6, 2020

Arrived in Maryland and my daughter is running late; it is so humid outside, and my phone is almost totally out of juice, so I decided to step back inside the airport to wait for her. There are so many entrances to enter the airport, and as fate would have it, I chose the entrance that has a dime on the other side of it. Angels are amazing. The area was all empty except for one single Pepsi vending machine. I quickly walked over to it to get to the outlet to charge my phone enough so that I would not miss my daughter's call, and as I was squatting to get to the outlet there, beside the vending machine was a dime, and I knew my father was with me. I am so happy! Yes, I took a picture.

Found a Dime

July 8, 2020

Angelo drove me to 1909, and I had to see the inside of the house one more time because last time I was living in this house, life was normal as we knew it—"before coronavirus." As I entered through the garage door, the first room I saw was the family room, just the way we left it, and there next to the sliding glass door, I found a shiny dime, and I knew my father was in the house too. It made me feel happy inside. Yes, I took a picture.

Angel Watching over Home

July 8, 2020

I stepped outside to see the backyard, and I was so happy that the vine that came up every summer was there! I had forgotten about this vine and how beautiful it was. It was so beautiful that I had to take a picture of it and FaceTime Geo to let him see it. I love nature. Well, it wasn't until nineteen days later that I was looking through my album and saw three white lines on the concert so I zoomed in to see what it was, and I saw an angel. There is an image of an angel right near and under the vine, my first thought was angels are watching over my son Cody who is still living in the house. God is amazing. Angels are amazing. Thank you watching over my son.

Son's Address No. 4

July 8, 2020

I'm spending the night at my eldest son's home this evening; my younger son drove me there, and as we were pulling up on this long and rocky road, I see a small white house, and as we get closer, I see the number 4 on the house. I knew his address before, but it never really dawned on me until now. Angel 4 is also watching over my eldest son. I am so very happy. Yes, I took a picture. Angels are amazing. Amen.

Sign I Am Returning Home

July 9, 2020

As my son is driving me to my mother's house for my last night in Maryland, a car slowly pulled up right next to us, which caught my attention. As it slowly passed by, I noticed the Arizona license plate on it, and I know it is a sign from spirit that I will be leaving for home soon. So amazing are the angels. Yes, took a picture.

Dinosaur at Carwash

July 12, 2020

Geo and I go through the carwash almost daily, and today after the wash, Geo wanted to vacuum and blow out the inside of his car. As I am helping him, I see a little green dinosaur on the ground next to the side of the car. Oh my God, I automatically know it is a sign and validation that my grandson is coming to visit me. He loves dinosaurs. I placed the dinosaur on our dash and took a picture and sent it to my daughter.

Found a Dime

July 15, 2020

Feeling a little worried because the governor of California has closed down the state because of COVID-19, restaurants that are operating are "carry-out services only." We are hungry and craving Red Lobster; I walked into the restaurant to place my order; the place is empty. I then proceeded the walk up to the counter where I saw a dime next to the "Please stand six feet apart" sticker on the floor. I automatically feel better that my father is here with me. Thank you, Dad, for loving me. Yes, I took a picture.

God's Promise

July 16, 2020

It is evening time, and I needed some cheap supplies from the dollar store. As I am walking around, I see two full boxes of calendars for 2021; the box on the left says "2021 kittens" and the box on the right says "2021 God's promise." I know this is a sign for me. Roscoe, our furry member of our family who gave us unconditional love, passed away last November, and I was so heartbroken. One day maybe a year from now, after my heart has fully recovered, I want to bring in a cat into my life again. I wanted a black kitten, and I was looking but not in the mood to buy; it was too early for me. I knew it was a message from above that 2021 was going to be the year I was to receive a kitten, so I stopped all my thoughts of cats until now. I then proceeded to the register with my items and the only register open was register no. 4, and the young lady's name tag read "Angel"! I cannot make this stuff up! God is amazing! Angels are amazing! Yes, I took a picture.

Dinosaur Sticker

July 18, 2020

My daughter and her family just landed, and as they are exiting the plane, my grandson finds a dinosaur sticker! It's just like when I found a little dinosaur at the carwash to confirm that they were indeed coming. I know that is a sign from above to confirm that they arrived safely. My daughter sent me a picture. He is so excited; he loves dinosaurs. He has everything dinosaur. My grandson was so happy to find it too. Thank you, angels, for watching over them. Angels are amazing.

Italian Deli Angel 4

July 18, 2020

We picked up Vanessa, Hollice, and Hunter from the airport, and everyone is hungry; I want Vanessa to try a rice ball, an Italian dish that takes hours to make, but I know this place in Scottsdale that is the only place that I know that sells them.

As Vanessa and I go inside to order, I, again, get concerned at all the masked people that I see, and I begin to worry a little; I then see Angel 4 walking around inside the market with us, and I knew the angels are around us. I feel safe again. Thank you, angels. Angel are amazing. Yes, I took a picture.

Happy Birthday, Dad

July 24, 2020

Today would've been my father's eighty-third birthday! My daughter took Geo's car to go watch the sunset with her family at the golf course. I went to the grocery store to get some treats and supplies to make cookies for my grandson for when he returned. When I came back outside, it got really windy, and it looked like a storm was coming. I forgot a greeting card but didn't want to go back inside, so I decided to go to Walgreens, which was around the corner, in and out, I told myself. I came out of the store, and it started to drizzle; I had not seen rain since March. I decided to say a special prayer for my father, and then I sang "Happy Birthday" to him in Italian as I drove home. I pull up and park, and as I am grabbing the bags out of the trunk, it starts to really rain hard! I quickly got inside and started unloading the groceries and then started to prepare the cookies when something told me to go outside on the deck.

I sat on the chair and watched and listen to the rain; it was peaceful. I then grab my phone went into Pinterest and looked up singing "happy birthday" in Italian, so I could hear it again; it reminded me of yesterday when I was a child. Moments later a rainbow appeared, and I knew it was a sign from my father. I love you, Dad. I am happy that you are my dad. *Buon compleanno* (that means "happy birthday" in Sicilian). Yes, I took a picture.

Hail Begins to Fall

August 1, 2020

A good friend of mine from Florida, Paul, was visiting me for a few days. We had not seen each other in four years. Since that time, his wife, Donna, had passed; both his wife and my father are very strong spirits. We are heading to Sedona today. I wanted to show Paul all the beauty that God has created out there, so along with my daily prayers, I asked God if we could receive a big sign from my dad and Donna too.

As we are driving there, I told Paul that I asked Donna and my dad for a special sign today. We finally arrived in Sedona; there was so much traffic that it took us an extra hour to get there. We are now ready for lunch. We head to the Wildflower Bread Company for a quick bite to eat. The day is nice with a few gray clouds, and so we sat outside as usual. As we are enjoying our lunch, I noticed a drop of rain hit my arm. I told Paul who is sitting across from me, and we continued eating.

A few minutes go by, and a few more drops of rain fall and now Paul also felt them. I checked the forecast, and no rain is forecasted. We continued to eat when it starts to slightly drizzle, and Geo said to Paul if he wanted to move inside. Paul said he is okay, but if it gets heavier, we can move. A few more minutes went by, and it started to RAIN. We quickly got our food and moved to a table that is still outside but sheltered from the rain. As we were enjoying our lunch and listening to the rain, it started to pour down rain, and then it turned to hail… Oh my god, it is hailing, and it is well over 100 degrees! Hail is falling all over the deck flooring. What a blessing of sign from above; my father and Donna are amazing. God is *amazing*. Yes, I took a picture and a video too. I love you, Dad, thank you.

Another Sign of Love

August 1, 2020

We are out in God's country, walking the natural trails that God has created through the mountains. The skies over the Sedona mountains are so blue and bright as the hot, hot sun shone upon us. We decided to sit down and soak it all in. I love to pray out here also. I feel a close connection to God, so I said a little prayer. We talked and took a few pictures, and before we know it is 7:15 p.m. and the sunset is on its way. It's time to head home.

As we are driving home, the colors of the evening skies are just breathtaking; the shades of orange, pinks, and the yellows and blues—God is the greatest artist in the world. We then all saw it, a small rainbow just a perfect way to end the day, and another sign from above that my dad and Donna are with us in spirit, amen. Yes, I took pictures.

A Fortune from Bazooka

August 5, 2020

We just dropped off Paul at the airport, and as Geo was pulling away, we start texting each other goodbye again, and I told him to call me when he lands. It has now been twenty-five minutes, and we are still driving home. I pulled out a piece of my favorite gum with a fortune attached, Bazooka, to wet my palate. I sometimes read the fortune and sometimes not, depending on my mood. Well, I decided to read the fortune today because Paul left, and I was sad.

The fortune reads, "ONE TRUE FRIEND IS WORTH A DOZEN FALSE ADMIRERS."

I automatically know it's a message from spirit to me; they are telling me he is a real deal, a true friend. Yes, I took a picture, and I sent it to him and Terry my friend and psychic/medium also.

Found a Dime

August 25, 2020

Babysitting today! Getting ready to take all four grandsons out for a walk to the playground, which is right up the street. After getting the stroller unfolded and ready, I test drive it to the end of the driveway to see that everything is okay before I put my grandson in it, and there at the end of the driveway I see it, a dime. It lay parallel to the driveway closer to the grass area, and I know that my father will be walking with us. I love you, Dad. It makes my heart smile. Yes, I took a picture.

Found a Dime

August 26, 2020

Cody's birthday! We spent the night at Skyler's house; Cody said we could sleep in his bed while he took the sofa—what a nice son. It is a queen bed, so Connor, Hunter, and I all slept together. In the morning, while we were fixing the fitted sheet that had come undone in the middle of the night, we found a dime on the bare mattress, and I knew my father was with us in spirit today celebrating Cody's birthday with us. I love you, Dad. Yes, I took a picture.

Special Message from a Friend

August 27, 2020

While waiting at the airport for my trip to Maryland on Sunday, I was writing all the great things that I shared growing up with my aunt. Well, tomorrow is her funeral, and when I woke up this morning, the song "You Are So Beautiful to Me" by Joe Crocker was in my head because I wanted to use it for tomorrow with the eulogy. The words describe my aunt. As I was reading the lyrics off the internet to see if they were okay, I received a Snapchat message from an ex-co-worker that sent me to tears. It reads:

"Good morning, just wanted to say I miss you, I love you, and to give you a bit of encouragement for the day. You are a ray of sunshine, and you peak through any rain cloud. Stay the positive happy you that you are, no matter who tries to rain on your parade."

No one at my old job knew that my aunt passed away. Angels are amazing. Amen.

Found a Dime

August 27, 2020

Today is my aunt's viewing: 2:00 to 4:00 p.m. and 6:00 to 8:00 p.m. It will be the very last day that I will ever see my aunt in the flesh. Vanessa, Conner, and I pay our respects. My aunt looks so beautiful. I kneel before her and say my prayers, and I touch her hand one last time. At 4:00 p.m., we all have to leave and there is a two-hour window before we can come back again for the second viewing. My cousin says they are having light refreshments at her home. At first, we decline because my grandson wants fast food, and then twenty minutes into the ride, my cousin leaves a voicemail asking us to please come over so we turn around and head to her home. On the way there, a thought comes into my head that I want to have one of Zia Lina's dresses (that's all she ever wore in the forty-nine years that I knew her) to remember her by, but I did not know how to ask the question. We all shared a quick light meal, and my cousin was asked about our aunt's final moments alive.

Once she had finished telling everyone what had happened, she said something about Zia Lina's dresses out of the blue, and I knew that was a message for above to jump in, and I asked if I could have a dress as a memory of her. Angels are amazing. My mother, Vanessa, and I followed my cousin upstairs to a closet full of dresses, and we were allowed to pick out the ones we wanted. I took three. It was now time to leave to be on time for the 6:00 to 8:00 p.m. viewing. We thanked our cousin and proceeded to exit her home. Vanessa was six steps in front of me. As I was walking, I could see something very shiny where I was walking toward, and I quickly called out, "Vanessa, Vanessa" and pointed to the shiny object and said, "A dime!" She walked toward it as I was coming up to it too, and I knew it was a sign from above. The only thing was, did my father send a dime, or did my aunt send the dime because she was happy that I wanted a dress of hers as something special to always look at and think of her? Yes, I took a picture.

Angel 44 Takes Me Home...

August 31, 2020

Today is the day I return home. Vanessa dropped me off at the airport. As I begin my walk toward gate B3, I see a large red crab with white numbers "44" on it and it makes me smile. I know that Angel 44 is with me. I stopped and took a picture. The restaurant is called Obrycki's. I continued to walk and finally arrived at gate B3 where I sat and waited for boarding for almost an hour. I noticed that the board has not changed to relay this; it still reads "Atlanta," so I get up and check with the woman behind the counter, and she told me at first that the flight for Arizona has already left, and I started to panic and say, "That cannot be." My boarding pass says 6:20 p.m. and it's only 6:00 p.m., she rechecks it and then says flight to Arizona is at gate A4 (for me that stands for Angel 4) and boarding is at 6:20 p.m. I thank her and quickly head over to gate A4. I know I will have a safe flight, Angel 4 is with me. Amen.

Found a Dime

September 3, 2020

Geo and I head to Sedona for the day. I love the peace that I feel when I am out there. We decided to take a walk under the bridge. There is a trail that is less than a mile long, and at the bottom, there is a running stream. As we proceeded to walk the trail, there is barbed wire between pillars so one does not go off trail. As we were walking, with me leading the way, a very small and shiny piece of silver caught my eye. It is over on the other side of the pillar. I cannot believe it! It's a dime! I quickly pointed it out to Geo who is directly behind me, and he saw it too. I crutch down and put my arm slowly through the barbed wire and retrieved it. Thank you, Dad, for continuing being a part of my life thirty years later. I love you. Yes, I took a picture.

"Luck 4"

September 23, 2020

We were driving home from Sedona, and I wanted to get another betta fish; this would make four, and I thought to myself, "Four is my angel number." I also want to stop by the Dollar Tree to get another scarecrow decor for our home. As Geo rode into the parking lot, I noticed Angel 4 was with us. The license plate read "LUCK 4." OMG! I cannot make this stuff up. Angels are always around us. Thank you, angels, for all your love and support you send us every day. Yes, I took a picture.

Angel at Horseshoe Bend

September 29, 2020

We took a day trip to see Horseshoe Bend in Page, Arizona. Another beautiful creation God has made. As we are taking in all this beauty, I noticed an angel on the side of the canyon. The angel is so beautiful—the wings, face, body, I cannot stop admiring the beauty that God has made. Yes, I took a picture. Angels are everywhere. Amen.

Helicopter Ride

September 30, 2020

Woke up in Utah, and Geo said, "I have a surprise for you, but we have to rush." Got dressed and out the door we went driving at top speeds to get there, but I did not know where we were going, except for Geo telling me where to turn left and right. Finally I see it: a helicopter with its propeller spinning. Geo is taking me for a helicopter ride—how exciting! At the same time, I'm scared of crashing, so I say a prayer to myself for angels to watch over us while we are up in the sky.

We got to see the mountains of Utah from way, way above, and we took pictures and videos also. What a view! After the ride was over, we decided to take more pictures of the beautiful scenery that was around us, and that's when I saw Angel 4. Angel 4 was at the entrance/exit of the place we were at. It was a dune buggy that advertised for the helicopter company that we took a ride on. I could not tell because the dune buggy was facing forward when we pulled into the place, but on leaving, I saw the number 4 on the back of the bumper, and I knew angels were watching over us in the sky. Yes, I took a picture.

BESAFE1

October 8, 2020

In Vegas, and we are heading to a place that I do not really like so I said a prayer for safety. As we were walking toward the car, I received a reply from the angels on the license plate that reads "BESAFE1," and I knew that the angels heard my prayers. Thank you, angels. Yes, I took a picture.

Four of Spades

October 9, 2020

Looking for Geo! Nor Robert (Geo's poker friend visiting) or Geo are in the poker room, and Geo handed me his dead phone when I dropped both of them off at the Caesar's Palace Casino, and I headed back to our hotel over an hour ago. This really frustrated me because I do not know where to look for them now, so I called Robert and he said that he was knocked out of the tournament and left forty-five minutes ago, but Geo was still in. So I decide to walk the whole casino with no luck and decided to go back to the hotel room; maybe we just missed each other and he was heading back to the room. As I was heading back, I said a little prayer to Penelope to help me find Geo. I approached the crosswalk along with others, stopped and waited for the light to change, and then started to walk diagonal across to our hotel; there, lying on the street, was Angel 4 (four of spades) playing card, and I knew that Penelope had heard my prayers. Yes, I took a picture and headed up to the room; minutes later, Geo showed up! Penelope, you are amazing. Angels you are amazing.

"One Day"

October 17, 2020

As I was driving to the grocery store, I was praying to God and asking him why I'm not happy. I was living in Arizona, my dream has come true, but then, why am I not happy? I pulled in the parking lot and proceeded to look for a spot to park when I received my answer, "ONE DAY." Immediately, I felt the love of Jesus inside of me, and I knew right away that he had answered my prayers. I started to cry. You know me; normally, I would take a picture immediately, but because I was in a rush and thought to myself, *I am only going into the store to grab a few items*, so I should be out well before the person that owns that car will be out.

Well, an hour and a half later here, I come out of the store with phone ready to take a picture, and the car is gone. I'm so upset at myself for not taking a picture when I first saw the car. I am now in my car about to drive away, as I circle the parking lot to pull out, I noticed a license plate that reads "TB2GOD." I know this is another sign for me. I took a picture and directly across is Angel 44 confirming. As I was driving home, I decided to speak into the microphone to record what just happened to me so I will not forget any details; as I was speaking, I see Angel 44 on the side of the road, and I know the angels are confirming what just happened again. Amen, Lord, amen. "I am happiest when I am serving." I realize that now. Thank you, Lord.

"Second Chance"

October 18, 2020

Was heading to the store, and I had to make a U-turn, but the sign read "no U-turns," so I drove up to the left-hand turn area where I was allowed to make a U-turn, but because the cars were approaching at such a fast speed, I decided to just make a left turn instead and then circle back around. As I was circling around, I noticed that the street was called Commonwealth Ave. (haha), and because I liked the style of homes, I wanted to videotape to show my mother the homes in Arizona. As I was driving around the circle very slowly and videotaping, I saw it! I saw it! I just saw the car with the license plate "ONE DAY."

This is the car that I tried to take a picture of the license plate yesterday, but because I was rushing, I did not take one. My first thought was this is a sign from the angels, and they are giving me a second chance at taking a picture of this license plate. Thank you, angels, for giving me another chance. Yes, I took a picture. God is amazing! Angels are amazing! God bless them.

Red Truck 044

October 27, 2020

We just entered Mexico! Geo and I wanted to see the ocean, so we decided to take a day trip there. We are a quarter of a mile in when we are flagged down by a uniformed police officer who is standing in the middle of the road with a machine gun and signals us to pull over. I quickly asked Geo if he was driving over the speed limit, he replies no and adds that he is only doing between 20–25 mph. The police officer, who does not speak any English is trying to tell us that Geo was speeding and he was caught doing seventy-plus miles per hour. Geo is trying to argue with him and tell him that he is wrong but the officer keeps showing him the radar gun, which says seventy-one. The officer also is trying to tell him that he can pay $50 now or he can go to the station and pay $100. At this point, Geo is furious and trying to call the man a liar. Since there is a lack of communication, and I want to try to defuse the situation, I try to intervene because I speak Sicilian and some of the words are similar. I tried to tell the police officer that maybe his radar gun is not working properly, but the officer tells me the same thing. The police officer then makes a phone call on his cell phone and hands it to Geo who refuses to touch it because of COVID-19 is going around and is being rude. I get out of the car and take the phone to listen to whoever is on the other end, thinking it's someone that speaks fluent English. It is not! It is another man who is saying the same exact thing as the officer. I again try to explain to the man on the phone that we were not speeding. As I was speaking with the man on the phone, the officer walked over to me and started pointing his radar gun at cars that were driving by and showed me their speeds. I now believe the officer and that his radar gun was properly working. As he finished showing me this, I looked up at the very exact moment that a very red 18-wheeler was *slowly* driving past our car with the only numbers on it, 044!

OMG! Angel 4 was with us! I wished at that very moment I had my phone with me to take a picture with, but the phone was in the car. Next thing I knew was the officer said to me what sounded like,

"You can go. You can go," and he smiled. Angels are amazing. I got into the car and told Geo, "I think he is letting us go." The officer moved away, and we proceeded to leave. Geo was very happy and thanked me, and I told him it was Angel 44 not I. I also told him, "Did you see the red tractor trailer that slowly crept up next to you while you were waiting for me? That truck had 044 written on it." He did not. Thank you, angels. I am so blessed to have you in my life. We found out later that the speed limit in Mexico is measured in kmh not mph like in America; it was our mistake.

We ended up staying the night because the boarder closes at 8:00 p.m. because of COVID, and we did not know that. The following day, we had to cross the border again to leave; we saw the same two men again, and Geo handed then a $20 bill to buy themselves lunch.

Found a Dime

October 31, 2020

Happy Halloween! Our first Halloween in the state of Arizona, and we decided to dress up in costumes and go out on the town! We decided we are going to try a different tavern to grab some lunch and watch some football action. As we were heading to the tavern, I'm thinking about getting another betta fish, and seconds later, Geo said, "Let's get a new betta fish." He is reading my mind again, scary.

Change of plans, we decided to head to the pet store before we go get lunch. We head to the betta section of the pet shop, and we started looking at all the pretty bettas. It seemed like it took forever because they are all unique. Ahhh, I finally picked one that we like and proceeded to purchase it, and then as I was heading out the double doors, there on the gray carpet, I saw a very shiny dime! I am so happy. I ran over, picked it up and kissed it. I knew my father is spending a minute with me, for it is Halloween. I then put the dime back on the floor along with the new betta I just purchased and took a picture. I love my dad.

Happy Halloween with a Dime

October 31, 2020

Geo and I are walking through the town of old Scottsdale taking all the sights. Geo is getting many laughs because people keep coming up to him and saying the cutest things because he is dressed up as a priest; one man even got on his knees and said, "Oh, Father, please forgive me," as we are walking and looking at all the exhibits there, I saw a dime on the sidewalk. I quickly pointed it out to Geo. I'm so excited my father is walking around with us; it's my first Halloween away from all my kids and my grandkids so this made my heart smile. Thank you, Dad, for loving me. Yes, I took a picture.

Heart of an Angel

November 2, 2020

We're headed to CVS because Geo wanted to print some photos to frame and give as gifts. When we arrived, I told him to go ahead of me because I wanted to finish my prayers before I went in. I finished my prayers and opened the door to get out, the sky was so bright and cloudy at the same time, which caused me to look up, and there I saw a beautiful angel looking at me with her arms extended and a heart of gold in the center. She was so beautiful, I could not take my eyes off her. I felt good inside, for I felt she had heard my prayers. Angels are amazing. I feel blessed; thank you, angels. Yes, I took a picture.

Angel Appears on Plate

November 9, 2020

We just arrived in Sedona, the air is crisp, and there is a light snow fall in the air, and I am excited. I just got my salt lamp! I asked Geo if he wanted to get lunch since it was a two-hour drive to get up here, and he said yes. We drive to Hideaway House, which is only minutes away from where we are and sit at the bar, and I decided to try something different, the brick chicken with vegetables. Geo had the usual, an order of fries, as we are waiting for our lunch. "You Could Do Magic" by America came on the radio, and my first thought is if this song is a sign for me. As the song comes to an end, our food arrived, and we started to eat, enjoying every bit of it. As I am finishing up my chicken, I noticed the leg resembles an angel? It is an angel! So beautiful there on my plate, and I knew it was a sign from spirit. I quickly showed Geo, who agreed. God is amazing. Angels are amazing. Yes, I took a picture.

White Feather

November 12, 2020

We are approaching Roscoe's first anniversary of his passing; I took his canister where I keep his ashes and brought it inside the apartment. I like to keep his ashes on the deck because he always loved laying in the sun and periodically I like to clean and refresh the words on the lid because the sun fades them away. Well, today, Roscoe made me smile; there was a tiny white feather stuck to his lid, and I felt it was a message of love from him. White feather meaning, "Your angel is here." I love you, Roscoe, forever in our hearts. Yes, I took a picture.

Penelope Appears

November 22, 2020

After dinner, I started to clean up the kitchen; the stove is always the last thing I spray and wipe clean. I sprayed the whole stove and proceeded to wipe all the surface with a paper towel I had in hand; as I'm wiping down the surface of the stove, I noticed what looks like a silhouette of Penelope. It is Penelope! My first thought was she is watching over us and blocking all of the negativity around us. I quickly showed Geo. I clean all the surfaces every day, and Penelope's silhouette still remains; it is like it is tattooed into the surface. The image of her then remained and it was still there on the last day we were there.

I am so happy that she is watching over us. Thank you, Penelope. Yes, I took a picture.

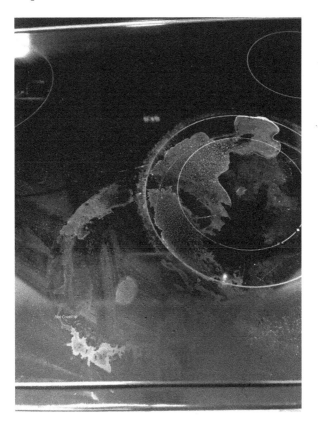

Black Bird Flying

November 27, 2020

I am driving to the grocery store to pick up a few items for dinner, and at the same time, I was thinking about where to buy my lottery tickets and the new area I really want to move to. We put in an application a few days ago and now are waiting to see if we got accepted. As I'm driving, something black caught the corner of my right eye, so I turned to look and it's a black bird flying parallel to me and keeping up with me too. I have to have a second look; I can see the bird's eyeball and all the details on its body clearly; this goes on for a few seconds. The bird even turned its head and looked at me, and it even looked like it's smiling at me, and I know it's a sign!

The first thing that comes to my mind is both the lottery and new apartment. Am I going to win the lottery tonight, or am I going to get approved for the new apartment? Later that evening, we received an email from the new apartment complex that our application was accepted. God is amazing. I wish I had a picture of the bird flying alongside me. Angels are amazing! Thank you for your continued blessings.

Gift Shop

December 1, 2020

We just arrived in Vegas, checked in, and now headed to our room to place our belongings. As we were walking toward the elevator, I noticed that there are miniature shops all around the area but continued walking to get on the elevator to take us to our room. After getting settled in, we decided to head out on the town. As we came out of the elevator and took a few steps, I noticed a black football jersey in the window of one of those miniature shops that we passed by on our way to the elevators with number 4 on the back and the number 4 on the sleeve but at an angel in which I see it, I see Angel 44. This made me smile and felt good inside, knowing that Angel 44 is with us. From then on, every time we went to our room or left the room, we were greeted by Angel 44. What a blessing. Angels are amazing. Yes, took a picture.

Vegas Magazine

December 1, 2020

We are in the parking garage of our hotel in Vegas. Walking to our car, we were all alone, and it was unkempt, and I did not feel safe here at all. As we continued to walk, I noticed a magazine lying on the ground all by itself. As I walk toward it to get to our car, I noticed the number 44 on the cover, and I knew Angel 44 was watching over us. Yes, I took a picture.

Vanessa Sends Me an Angel

December 7, 2020

I need a doctor's order to get my mammogram done. I sit in my car and call urgent care and explain my situation; they can see me today. Thank you, angels, thank you, angels. I drive over there to get a checkup and a doctor's order for a mammogram as I'm walking out I get a Snapchat picture from my daughter, Vanessa. It's a picture of popcorn, and I can see an angel in it. The angel is in prayer mood. I know that everything will be okay. Thank you, angels. Angels are amazing. Yes, I took a picture.

Happy Birthday, Angel

December 11, 2020

Happy birthday to me! I turn fifty today. I want to have lunch in Sedona, get myself a crystal, and walk on the mountain trail to celebrate. I know the exact crystal I want; it's a sun-shaped crystal, which I saw at the crystal shop where I bought my salt lamp. We arrived at the gem store, and I purchased the sun crystal and another crystal that caught my eye—both so beautiful. I head outside and then decided to enter in again to look around to see if anything else catches my eye. As I am looking around, I see a basket of my favorite orange citrate stones. I know that I already have all that I need, but I decided to see if any of them caught my eye as I examined each piece I come across a piece that has a white angel facing me. I could feel her love for me; she is so beautiful. I know this is a gift from heaven above. I walked up to the man behind the counter to purchase the stone. I tell him that it's my birthday today and look at the angel that I found on the stone. It's a gift from above, so I need to buy it. He smiled at me and replied, "You can have it." What a beautiful man. I held his hand and thanked him. God is amazing; angels are amazing. Yes, I took a picture.

Black Bird for Protection

December 18, 2020

Geo was outside our apartment when he noticed a dead black bird on the very top of the tree; somehow, the bird had a stick through it as though it had not seen it and flew right into it. The tree hung toward our deck; my first thought was it is a sign of protection for us because of the negativity that surrounded us since we moved here, and we have had enough. It also reminds me of *The Ten Commandments* movie when the blood of the lamb was put over the doors of the newborns that were to be saved. Thank you, angels, for watching over us. I feel protected.

The black bird corpse stayed in that tree until the very last day when I handed in the keys, February 2021. Yes, I took a picture.

(A black feather is a sign of protection, and we had over one hundred of them because the bird was all black.)

Angel Is My Answer

December 28, 2020

Earlier in the day, after watching *Highway to Heaven*, I went over to the picture of Jesus that hangs on our wall and asked him in prayer if I was an earth angel. I want to see a sign. It is now around 8:30 p.m., and we are having dinner at the Blue Coyote, a restaurant inside of Talking Stick Casino. As I am finishing up my dinner of a half-baked potato, half a steak, and asparagus. I noticed an angel praying on my plate. It is my answer to my question. I began to cry. I love you, Jesus. Yes, I took a picture. Amen.

About the Author

Her name is Maria, and she lives in the great state of Arizona with her domestic partner, Geo, and her cat Utah.

Milton Keynes UK
Ingram Content Group UK Ltd.
UKHW051453081223
434030UK00022B/284